PUT ON SOME CLOTHES AND ACT LIKE A DOCTOR

A FIELD GUIDE TO GROW YOUR PRACTICE FOR CHIROS, PTS, AND ANYONE WITH AN INDEPENDENT MEDICAL PRACTICE

MARK SCRIBNER

Practicefixers.com

First Printing, October 2022

To my wife Jaime-

It was your sacrifice at home that allowed me the time to learn these things.

Thanks for always being my Number 1 fan. I love being us!

You sure are good people.

Mark has done a great job in this book of outlining actionable steps for practice improvement applicable to all private practitioners in the healthcare world. His decades of experience in this area becomes quickly obvious. He uses pithy examples and anecdotes to his get his point across which makes the book a good read. His practical advice in a variety of topics from social media and marketing to new streams of revenue is nothing short of fantastic. If you're thinking about opening up a practice or even if you've been in already in practice; whether you're just starting out or have an established practice, this book is a must read.

    Dr. Charlie Rasmussen, D.O. , AAFP

    Physician / Owner TableRock Family Medicine

    Branson, MO

I've opened three physical therapy practices and know from experience that Mark hit the nail on the head with this book. I just wish he had hit ME in the head with this 15 years ago. This book is filled with practical and reliable ideas to help you no matter where you are in your practice development. Bury yourself into this book and take his advice. You won't be sorry.

    Dr. Brian Sundahl, DPT, OCS, CSCS

    Owner of Endeavor Physical Therapy

    Damascus, OR

I have owned my PT practice for 30 plus years and had the pleasure of working with Mark. He is truly the wizard behind the curtain that makes a practice or any business successful. His book is a fun easy read that can be your blueprint to success.

    Robert Chapman, PT

    Owner of Sunlakes Physical Therapy and Rehab

    Warsaw, MO

"People often forget that healthcare is a business and it must be well managed in order for patients to succeed. Being personally present for a lot of these stories, I can only encourage readers to digest the information and understand the reality in this book is coming for you whether you like it or not. Use this book like an encouragement, a constant, a training source, and a reminder that the best is yet to come."

Dr. Brittany Wright, DPT, FMT-C, MFR, CCI, SFMA
Owner of Wright Rehab and Wellness
Nixa, MO

I've been in practice for over 20 years, managed clinics, and worked in several private and larger corporation Physical Therapy clinics.

Mark shoots straight in this book, covering a wide variety of issues and topics that are common problems that both limit how well a company runs in the day to day and how much growth it can experience. It contains simple and straight forward advice that I wish I heard at the beginning of my career.

I've had the pleasure to be around and work with Mark over many years. He has a unique ability to organize and put structure in place for great success. He is a pleasure to be around and you will be encouraged just by meeting him.

Brian Klamm, PT, MCMT, CKTP, CCI
Tonganoxie, KS

I completely endorse this book. Speaking from the last 34 years of experience in Health Care, I find the author to be poignantly accurate and practically informative in every chapter. I feel confident that the contents of this book will be as relevant today as in the years ahead, which is no easy task.

I've worked with Mark Scribner directly for upwards of 4 years now and seeing his performance as a Chief of Staff has been an pleasure to witness first hand. In a previous clinic I held this role of Chief of Staff in a multi-discipline clinic and know it can be a quite difficult task to balance revenue driving action with interpersonal management of various positions. The busier the clinic, the more there is to balance and do so gracefully and professionally. To see Mark in action reaffirms that a physician should stick to what he or she is good at, treating patients, and let the day-to-day management be left to the Mark Scribner's of the world.

Having the voice of this author paint the picture of what a clinic can look like under appropriate management was a pleasure to read. Whether you are a practitioner of 25 years or a newer professional looking to cut your teeth in the field, this book is for you. Do your future self a favor and lean in to learn from the best.

Dr. James E Hussey DC, CKTP, CVCP
Chiropractor and Former Chief of Staff
St. Charles, MO and Branson, MO

CONTENTS

I didn't write this book to be your friend. I wrote this book because my friend, Dr. Matthew Sams hired me years ago to help him turn around his practice, and together we did just that. It wasn't easy. It wasn't without some tears and it definitely wasn't without some really hard work. But we did it!

I hope this book will act as a field manual for you to clean up and grow, and eventually scale your practice. I hope that you are able to implement some of these ideas into your practice. I hope that some of these ideas help take the stress away from you that is causing you to not sleep well at night. I hope this little book will act as a money printing press for you and helps you with your long-term financial goals.

My goal is to give you quick and to-the-point ideas and a glimpse as to why we did them. You are more than welcome to disagree with me. You are more than welcome to say "no." You are more than welcome to think I'm crazy. You are more than welcome to let this book sit on your "to read" pile for months, but just remember, I'm not the one stressing about your business at night... you are.

Why not try some of these things? They
worked for us!

WHO AM I?

My name is Mark Scribner. Twenty-three years ago, I helped another doctor sell his practice to the doctor I am currently working for, Dr. Matthew Sams. Through many twists and turns, I am now working as a trusted adviser in the executive and daily operations of this same practice 23 years later.

I am passionate about helping people live a John 10:10 type of "life in all its fullness." Throughout my career, I have fulfilled that mission in an eclectic manner through business management, healthcare management, and pastoral roles. Currently, I am Chief of Staff at Healing Arts Center in Branson, Missouri, where I provide executive direction and oversight for this multi-specialty clinic.

I also help other practices do exactly what we are doing through practical oversight and consulting. I was tired of being marketed to by people who didn't know ANYTHING about running a medical office and especially a multi-specialty practice. I found myself coaching the coaches that I had hired to coach me. The deciding factor for me to start doing this was the day I was scrolling Facebook and I saw all these pictures of these so-called practice growth people who "used to be in practice" and now they "show others how". At the speed in which this industry changes, I thought to myself, why would I want to learn from someone who isn't still practicing or managing a practice?

Being married and having five children are some of the biggest blessings in my life. I am also an itinerant evangelist with a clothing ministry that gives out new clothing to those in need. Through many healthcare challenges of my own, including a near-fatal automobile accident in 2015, I have been a life-long student of holistic health and non-traditional treatments.

WHO IS THIS BOOK FOR?

Originally, when I started writing it, it was for chiropractors and physical therapists, but as I have talked with medical doctors and other clinic owners they all shouted, "We need that book too!"

FORMAT OF THIS BOOK.

This book will be anecdotal, practical, and to-the-point. At the end of some of the chapters, we will have some "What are you gonna do about it?" type of action steps. Some of the chapters are short, because in the words of Forrest Gump, "that's all I have to say about that."

CHAPTER 1

Winners Always Want the Ball!

I really wish we could just hang out for a few days and discuss what's going on with your clinic. We could go out for some great BBQ, swap medical office war stories, and get to know each other really well. Before we even got to your office, I think we would sit down and watch a movie. What movie, you ask? The 2000 blockbuster *The Replacements*. There are some great motivational lines in there that I would want you to hear from Coach McGinty, and I'm going to do my best to give some of my own throughout this book, but here are a few from Coach McGinty that you need to read before we start. Ready?

> *Jimmy McGinty:* Falco! If I had wanted Cochran to have the ball, I would've called it that way!

> *Shane Falco:* I read blitz.

> *Jimmy McGinty*: Bull$#!+!, I put the game in your hands... you got scared.

> *Shane Falco:* I READ BLITZ.

Jimmy McGinty: [walks over and looks at Falco with disgust]

Winners always want the ball... when the game is on the line.

It was through this short motivational scene from Coach that I patterned most of my business decisions for our practice. I realized that the only way to score major points is by keeping the ball. Yeah, you can get an occasional 2 points for some defensive moves, but the major points are when you are on offense.

Think about your practice for a minute.

If you think about the relationships, the patients, the staff, the finances, the decisions you make, and the decisions you don't make, you will realize that many of them are based upon defensive moves. You are allowing your practice to be completely run from the WRONG SIDE of the football. It's time to send Danny Bateman into the game, and this book is your Danny.

> Jimmy McGinty: [stopping Danny before he runs onto the field] *Danny, I need the ball.*
>
> Daniel Bateman: *You need the ball.*
>
> Jimmy McGinty: *I need you to get me the ball.*
>
> Daniel Bateman: *I'm going to get you the ball.*
>
> Jimmy McGinty: [starts shouting repeatedly to rev Danny up] *Are you gonna get me the ball!*

Daniel Bateman: [shouting back repeatedly] *I wanna get you the ball!*

[then runs on the field]

Well, Shane, I've got some great news for you today. Let's get you that ball back, put it in your capable hands, and let's start scoring some major points for your team!

ACTION STEPS:

What are the areas of your practice where you are making defensive moves vs. offensive moves?

Be decisive! If you don't make a decision, someone else will make it for you. It is always better to make an offensive move than a defensive one.

Never stop learning and advancing your skills. The best offense is a good defense. Stay up on the latest and greatest information, technology, and trends so you can be the best at what you do!

When you start making more offensive moves in your business, you will see a dramatic difference in all areas of your practice.

CHAPTER 2

Better Bring Your Umbrella

When we started unpacking the issues of the office and noticing the problems that we needed to fix, it was NOT the most pleasant of experiences! Quite honestly, it was downright scary. I remember many times, reminding Dr. Sams and his wife that "it was going to be okay." I kept having to do this as long-time employees were quitting or being fired. I kept having to do this as they were spending money on things they had never spent money on before. I kept having to do this as we upped our professionalism. I kept having to do this as I created policies and made the staff adhere to them.

I know this isn't scientifically correct, but this is the visual image I gave them:

Often Dr. Sam's wife Tricia and I would stand together shoulder to shoulder.

Me: "Close your eyes." (She would close her eyes) "Do you hear that?"

Her: "No"

Me: "It's the faint roar of a wave. An earthquake just happened deep in the ocean. This earthquake is all the work that we have started and will continue to do. Over the next several days, weeks, months, and years that roar is going to get louder. You are going to get scared. You are going to have to be ready for the power of what we started. There will be a day soon, when the roar is so loud that you will want to run. Your face will be wet with the spray of the ocean, but stand firm, we aren't going anywhere."

I get a kick out of how ready.gov answers the question: "How do you survive a tsunami if you are on the beach?"

> Drop, Cover, and Hold On. Drop to your hands and knees. Cover your head and neck with your arms. Hold on to any sturdy furniture until the shaking stops.

Often on this journey "the shaking" would stop, albeit temporarily. It wasn't uncommon that the owners would say to me, "I can't believe that worked out." I reminded them of this story:

In that year, there was no rain. There had been no rain for the third consecutive year. A swath of brown dusty rubble covered the land where the crops had disappeared. In the dusty distance, trees were silhouetted like cactus with leaves that had long since fallen. The village used to be skirted by a stream. There was no water in the riverbed now. The surface now resembled a checkerboard pattern with cracks as wide as a foot, where once flowed clean, fresh water from nearby mountains. In the meantime, vultures circled the town searching for carcasses of dead animals, but no one was sure what had happened to the birds.

The land was suffering from famine. Various international charities brought them rations to survive on as people walked around barefoot.

A huge banyan tree standing as old as the village was the site of a desperate meeting of the people of the village. A woman in her eighties said, "Let us pray. God is the only one who can help us at this time."

Among the people coming together for prayer, a little girl running with her younger brother, holding an open umbrella over their heads, came running from a nearby village. Their umbrellas still unfurled, they stood there huffing for breath. The crowd could not help but turn to see what was happening. Several people were irritated and even furious when the umbrella's spokes poked them.

"We are here to pray for rain, not to bring an umbrella! Aren't you aware that it is not raining? It would be foolish to stand outside with an open umbrella on such a clear night."

The two young siblings chimed in, "Yes, indeed." They added, "We came to pray as well. We feel confident that our prayer will be answered, and rain will fall. Therefore, we brought a large, colorful umbrella."

It's time Doc, for you to believe that you can do this with the help from others, and get out your umbrella!

ACTION STEPS:

What are you most afraid of regarding your practice?

>   Growth?

>   Too much growth?

>   Failure?

>   Losing Employees?

>>   Why?

>>   Which ones?

Have you been "praying for rain" in your practice? Are you really prepared if it does in fact rain?

CHAPTER 3

Holes in Your Medical Office Funnel

I remember my first day on the job as Chief of Staff. I wanted to get to know the staff better so I started with buying lunch for this one department. There were two of them in the department. I got their lunch order, picked it up, and met them in their area. I took the first bite of food and while I was chewing, one of them spoke up and said, "Just so you know, we are pissed off that you are here." I just kept chewing and I smiled. I let her finish her reasons as to why I was horrible. When she was finished, I just looked at her and kept smiling. She didn't like this. She asked me why I was smiling. I said, "All those things are actually not anything I created; I have only been here for 4 hours. So all these problems you are blaming on me were created by someone else."

I realized that this pointed out just how far we had to go in order to fix the problem. I realized that the staff was a festering boil just waiting to be lanced. But it was more than that! There were some major holes in our funnel!

Since I was a former youth pastor, I knew how to illustrate this to the staff in the form of a game. I went to Home Depot, bought four buckets and two large funnels. I drilled a bunch of holes in the funnels and, like something straight out of the show *Double Dare* on Nickelodeon, we did a relay race of transferring water from one end of the yard to the other by using the funnels. The only way for this to work was for the team to all use their fingers to plug these holes while walking together to the end of the course.

It's funny that looking back at this now, none of those people are on my team anymore, but more on that later.

This exercise was a good one because it shows many things. Mostly that you have to first identify that there are holes, and then you have to fill them.

I like submarine movies. My wife, not so much. In every submarine movie they take the submarine to "maximum depth" and then pipes rattle and shoot out water. Then someone comes in and clamps the pipes to fix the problem.

So what were these holes? You will read about them throughout this book. These holes are what make up the chapters of this book. Have we fixed these holes? Yes, many of them. Do some still pop up? Yep! What do we do? We clamp them and patch them. Sometimes we get wet.

That is what I hope to do with you in this book. Let's take you and your practice to maximum depth and see what holes pop up!

ACTION STEPS:

Do you have any known holes in your funnel currently?

    What are they?

    What are you doing to plug them?

    Do you need help fixing them?

Some of the categories of these holes in your funnel are:

SCHEDULING

- Confirming appointments
- No shows or cancellations
- Patient (non)compliance with treatment plans

RECEPTION AND CHECK-IN PROCESS

- Disengaged staff
- Patient satisfaction with wait times

FINANCIAL DISCUSSIONS AND COLLECTIONS

- Staff comfort level in having money conversations
- Provider communication and documentation
- Unclear or conflicting provider instructions to staff
- Inefficient workflows

EXTERNAL MARKETING

- Reputation management
- Online reviews and ratings

These are some of the most common holes in a medical office's funnel. By taking the time to identify and fix these holes, you can improve patient retention and satisfaction.

Take a look at your entire workflow and see where there might be some leaking water.

CHAPTER 4

Put on Some Clothes and Act Like a Doctor

There, I said it! Put on some clothes and act like a doctor! I get a kick out of many DCs and DPTs. They get irritated when someone finger air-quotes the word "doctor" when referring to their profession, but they show up to work in not much more than a t-shirt or tank-top and let people call them "Doctor Larry" or worse yet, just "Larry."

So what do your patients call you? I recommend they call you "Doctor (Last Name)."

What does your staff call you? I require that my staff call my doctors "Doctor (Last Name)." The 1995 movie *The American President* sums this up well:

> President Andrew Shepherd: *Two-ball on the side.* [He makes the shot, and the two-ball goes into the pocket]

> A. J. MacInerney (Chief of Staff): *Nice shot, Mr. President.*

> President Andrew Shepherd: *"Nice shot, Mr. President?" You won't even call me by my name when we're playing pool?*

> A. J. MacInerney: *I will not do it playing pool, I will not do it in a school. I do not like green eggs and ham, I do not like them, Sam I Am.*

Now here's where you can take this "name thing" a little bit too far. When out in public amongst other professionals and executives, the title may make you come across as pretentious. At the very least, give your first name too. Chiropractors, pastors, and academics seem to be the worst at this.

I was in a meeting recently with a D.C. (we'll call Dr. Pop McCracken) and a D.O. (we'll call Dr. Nothing Toprove). During introductions it went like this:

> Me: *I'm glad you all are here, have you met before?*

> D.O.: *Hello, my name is Nothing Toprove*

> D.C.: *Doctor McCracken*

They shake hands, the D.O. looks at me and leans in expecting to hear a name, but never gets it. I felt so awkward. The D.O. brought it up to me later and said, "What's his first name?"

Why in the world would you do this? This is a contemporary in your field, don't be that guy/girl!

Every time I think about this, I'm reminded of the scene in the 1985 movie *Spies Like Us* when Chevy Chase and Dan Aykroyd are pretending to be doctors and they all go back and forth saying, "Doctor", "Doctor", "Doctor", "Doctor", "Doctor", "Doctor", "Doctor", "Doctor", "Doctor"…

I walked into a chiropractor's office one day and the "Doctor" came out of his office wearing basketball shorts and a tank top. He said, "Are you ready?" I said, "For a pick-up game?" Come on Doc, dress the part.

I'm not saying you need to wear a white coat, though there is some amazing research that BMJ did in a 2018 survey about just that: (https://bmjopen.bmj.com/content/8/5/e021239) I am saying you should dress professionally. Ask yourself, what does my geographic region dictate in terms of what the "uniform" should be? I used to work at a rural church as a pastor in Kansas and my first few Sundays I wore a suit. This was in a farming area and it was definitely a "blue-jean" type of church. The people looked at me weirdly. I stopped wearing the suit, but kept the tie, because at the time, I was so young and I needed something to set me apart as someone with authority. However, not wearing a suit at a church on the east coast would not be acceptable. Know your area and know your patient base. Dress the part, but one step above.

For the Chiros reading this: We all know the schooling data. The typical D.C. goes to school for 4 years; the total time in formal schooling is around 7,200 hours. The typical M.D. spends closer to 10,000 hours in formal schooling, and a D.O. somewhere in between.

So does that make an M.D. or D.O. more intelligent than a D.C.? No, but it does make them more experienced in their field. And we need to act accordingly. You need to understand that as a Doctor of Chiropractic, you are not on an equal footing with an M.D. or D.O., in the eyes of the general public and in the eyes of other medical professionals. You are seen as an "alternative" provider. And that's okay, because that's what you are. You are not trying to be M.D.'s, you are not trying to be D.O.'s. You are Doctors of Chiropractic and you need to act like it.

I remember hearing a story about a chiropractor who was just starting out in the medical world. He said that he would walk into a room full of M.D.'s and D.O.'s and he would just get this feeling like he didn't belong. He said he felt like an imposter. He said it took him years to get over that feeling and to act like he belonged in that room. And that's what you need to do. You need to walk into a room full of M.D.'s and D.O.'s and act like you belong.

The bottom line is this: if you want to be taken seriously as a doctor, you need to act like one. You need to dress like one, talk like one, and walk like one.

I'm not saying that you need to put on a fake persona, but I am saying that you need to be professional. You need to be the best you that you can be. You need to rise to the occasion and meet people where they are at.

So, next time you walk into a room full of M.D.'s and D.O.'s, put on your best suit, shine your shoes, and act like the professional that you are.

To the PTs reading this: The same goes for you. Your schooling is different, your scope is different, but it is still an earned doctorate and you are still a professional and you need to act like it.

ACTION STEPS:

Are there areas of you practice where you need to start acting more professional?

What are they?

What can you do to change that?

Immediately:

Mid-term:

Here are some areas of professionalism in your office that you might need to take a look at fixing.

- You and your staff should be well-dressed and groomed at all times.
- Your office should be clean and organized.
- You and your staff should always be polite and courteous.
- You should always be on time for appointments.
- You should never discuss personal or confidential information about patients with anyone other than the patient or staff members who need to know.
- You and your staff should always be professional when dealing with insurance companies, lawyers, and other medical professionals.
- You should never miss appointments or cancel appointments without giving proper notice.
- You and your staff should always be honest with patients.
- You should always "do no harm."

CHAPTER 5

The Offer of Hope

I was in a really bad car wreck in 2015. I literally should be drinking from a straw and not walking, but by the grace of God (and many doctors and therapists), here I am doing quite well. I remember for about 14 months of my life I went to therapy or doctor appointments for 5 days a week. These people became my life; they were my friends, they were my family.

My grandfather, Lloyd Lewis, was diagnosed with Leukemia in 1989. He practically cured himself of Leukemia by reading the *Merck Manual* and the *Physicians' Desk Reference*. I remember him telling a story about when he "rang the bell" on the oncology floor at the hospital.

Here's how I remember him telling me this story. He told me that ringing that bell was one of the saddest days of his life. I asked him why and he said, "Because when I rang that bell, it meant that they were done with me; all that time I had invested in them, and all the friendships I had made with them. When I rang that bell, it meant I was done and they were done with me. I felt like I had no purpose, and no hope."

This story sat in the recesses of my mind until I was in my car wreck. Then I started going to different therapies. I remember when I would "graduate" from these therapies. It was so frustrating, because I wasn't actually all the way better; I was just improved enough to not need them. I kept telling them, "I'm not back to being me again." These people had never met me prior to my wreck, so they didn't know who the real "me" was.

I remember one time I had what looked like a pouch of non-crepitus subcutaneous air next to my rib cage and right above my diaphragm. It looked funny and felt even funnier. You could totally notice it from under a shirt. I asked the head of trauma surgery at the hospital what it was. He said, "We looked at it via ultrasound, and it is normal." "NOR-MAL?!?!?!?," I yelled. "This thing isn't normal." This doctor couldn't figure out what was wrong with me, so he told me I was normal. I literally had this pooch of something coming out of my stomach like a cantaloupe-sized goiter… and he calls it "NORMAL."

I then asked him, "Do you think there is someone in this world that is smarter than you?"

He didn't like that question, but he said, "I suppose so."

"Good," I said, "then I'm going to find them, and when I do, they are going to need my medical records. I need you to cooperate with them as we are finding out what is still wrong with me."

I took this story from my grandfather and my wreck and I started implementing it in our practice. We simply called it HOPE. It's not a fancy acronym or anything, it's just HOPE. I never wanted any of our patients to feel the way that I felt after my wreck when the doctors were done with me or couldn't find out what was wrong. We also didn't want patients, who we did get better, to feel like we were done with them.

So here it is: "You might have come here for chiropractic, acupuncture, nutrition, nurse practitioner, hearing instruments, physical therapy, IV therapy, hormone therapy, or weight loss, but we actually don't offer any of those services. The only service we offer is HOPE. HOPE that we are going to be with you through this entire journey. HOPE that if you need a care that we don't offer, that we will help you find it. HOPE that we will be here when you get back from there or have another injury or issue."

This is our message of HOPE. We tell it to our staff weekly. We remind our patients. He have it plastered on our walls and on T-shirts.

ACTION STEPS:

Have you ever had a long-time patient who you were able to get better and then you didn't see them for a while?

What is the message that your office is portraying to your patients about:

> Your longevity?

> Their importance?

Are you making them feel like "family" or are they just another number?

Would they be sad if you "kicked them out?"

CHAPTER 6

Image Matters

I actually have a background in graphic design and shirt printing. Quality Matters. In this chapter, we are going to quickly address these things.

When I worked at the church in Kansas, we did this massive re-branding from a vintage 60s logo to a relevant and timeless logo. I wanted to create an iconic image that you could use words on or just have the brand "icon" that eventually would become recognizable as the Brand.

Let us use McDonald's as an example. I remember the first time I took my kids to St. Louis to see the Arch. We had a competition in the car to see who could see the arch first. I knew we were a couple of minutes away and then all of a sudden, one of my youngest said, I see the arch... actually I see two of them. They had seen the Golden Arches of McDonalds and felt like they had won. I'll tell you, when my 3-year-old son saw our new church logo about a year after I had launched it and said, "My church," I knew that I had created a brand that even a 3-year-old could recognize.

We did the same for our medical practice. We started with an old logo, took some elements from it, modernized it, and then created an icon out of it. We put it on everything—shirts, signs, business cards, letterhead, watermarks, pens, and practically everything. I knew we had reached market saturation with the brand when I went to get gas on the other side of town and the gas station attendant saw my shirt and said to his co-worker, "That's where I go to the doctor. You should go see them." This guy didn't know me; he knew the brand. Your brand is important.

LOGOS

If you don't have a professionally designed logo, you need one. I'm not talking about one you designed in Microsoft Paint, but one you had properly typeset and vectorized. A good logo needs to be noticeable in color AND black and white. It needs to be noticeable in a fax. It needs to look good embellished on a shirt and a pull-over/jacket. It needs to represent you and your company.

If you don't have a quality logo, you don't have to spend a fortune on one. Some people really like the website fiverr.com for such things. A simple Google search will reveal innumerable artists ready, willing, and able to do your logo.

Once you have this new logo, be ready to re-brand your office. Freshen up your paperwork, signage, business cards, letterhead, EHR software... literally everything with your new logo.

There are many affordable options out there for inexpensive and quality printing.

UNIFORMS

I've already told you where I stand on what some of you are wearing to the office. Create a policy (and stick with it) on what your team is going to wear. At our office, we have different classifications of workers and different rules for each department for uniforms. I'll tell you what we do and you can tweak it for yourself.

Clinical Staff (Doctor's assistants who have direct patient care) – They wear a fitted black scrub with a solid color undershirt if needed. They also have a nametag.

Clerical Staff – Business professional attire with their nametag. They also have the option of wearing the same scrub as Clinical Staff. We aren't a pediatric office or a vet clinic, so we don't wear patterned scrubs!

Therapy Department – Mid-levels wear a specific color in a logoed athletic/yoga smock. Doctors wear a different color with the same logoed smock. Doctors also wear an embroidered athletic fit "white coat" when seeing a patient for the first time.

Chiro Department – Currently we only have two men. They wear a non-ripped designer jean or khaki pant and an embroidered polo shirt with the logo and their name (instead of a nametag). Of course, it says, "Dr. Last Name." Did you expect otherwise?

Medical Department – On clinic days we wear single-color scrubs. On office visit days, we wear business professional with a white coat when necessary.

Administration – Business professional, scrubs, or logoed polo shirts.

Why all the choices? Because different people have different body types. I wanted them to be comfortable and professional. Is this the best option for you? I don't know, I'm just telling you what we do.

One thing we don't do is: Have a casual Friday or dress up for Halloween. I remember one time going to a pharmacy on Halloween and the whole office was dressed up in costume... I'm talking dressed up. The main pharmacist was dressed up (or should I say dressed down) like a wench. I remember thinking, "If she lost some of my pills, I'm pretty sure I know what crevasse they fell down." I always think of the *Dilbert* comic entitled "Casual Day has gone way too far" and it shows the naked backside of a guy walking down the hall. It's easier for me to manage not doing a casual day by sticking with the uniform policy.

COPIES OF COPIES

While we are talking about how things look, you need to check your printed documents like intake forms, pain drawings, insurance forms, waivers, sign-in sheets, etc. Copies of copies need not be allowed. If you don't have the original, recreate it. Get the original documents to your staff and tell them to stop making copies of copies.

Last, but not least in this chapter is **typographical errors**. I literally was offered a job one time out of 120 candidates because my resume was THE ONLY ONE without any typos. This is because my dad used to pull out his red pen like an elementary school teacher and circle my spelling mistakes on ANYTHING and EVERYTHING I wrote, typed, or produced. I remember one time we were visiting a church on a Sunday and I was sitting next to him. I observed him circling the bulletin with grammatical and spelling mistakes. I now find myself doing the same thing. He doesn't know it yet, but he will be editing this book before it goes to press, so if you find any mistakes, it's his fault! *Professionalism, on all levels, matters!*

Check your documents. Check your EHR note templates. Check everything you produce and reproduce and make sure things are spelled correctly and that the correct grammar is used. If this isn't your thing, reach out to an English teacher and trade services.

ACTION STEPS:

Do you have a quality logo?

Does it look good in a fax?

Does it look good on a shirt?

What does your logo portray about your company?

What items do you want to see with your logo on it?

Are you happy with what your staff wears?

Are you happy with what your providers wear?

Are the things you and your staff wear portraying your image well?

What documents do you need to recreate and/or stop making copies of copies?

What public documents do you have that need to be looked at for typographical errors?

INEXPENSIVE WEBSITES TO GET PRINTING SERVICES:

Vistaprint – www.vistaprint.com
Overnight Prints – www.overnightprints.com
UPrinting – www.uprinting.com

INEXPENSIVE PLACES TO GET A LOGO:

Fiverr – www.fiverr.com
99designs – www.99designs.com
Design Crowd – www.designcrowd.com

PLACES YOU CAN ORDER AN EMBROIDERED POLO FROM:

Lands' End – www.landsend.com
Logo Sportswear – www.logosoftwear.com
Any Promo – www.anypromo.com

You probably have a place in your town that does embroidery. Google term: Embroidery Near Me

CHAPTER 7

What Are You Putting up With for $147?

Let me explain. When I was hired at my current job, I was tasked with many things, but the biggest task was to "turn around the Physical Therapy department." I didn't know what that meant, but I was ready to tackle anything.

The Physical Therapy department had been in operation for about 10 years prior to my arrival. Its first year out of the gate, 2006, it billed almost $450,000 and continued this for the next 3 years. Then in 2009, it took a drastic decline of around $160,000 to just over $290,000 per year. It then bounced back and forth as it declined to $180,000 the year before I arrived in 2017.

Why did it do this? There were several reasons, which I will lay out for you in this chapter, but to go quickly to the answer it was primarily STAFF and MANAGEMENT that caused this. The 2009 dip could have been partially credited to the Affordable Care Act, but not in its entirety. Again, I maintain, it was STAFF and MANAGEMENT... prior to my arrival.

I promise I'm not making any of this stuff up. Some of these parts I witnessed myself, and some I just have the legendary stories I was told. When I arrived, the clinic was busy, but very unorganized. This lack of organization lead to some management issues we will deal with, but you need to know this because the department was basically running itself into the ground.

When I arrived, the department was operated by a 3/4 time PT and a full-time PTA. They had proven in year's past that they actually could run a successful and busy clinic, but that wasn't the case when I arrived. Before I go any further, these two individuals, when they wanted to be, were very talented and very good at their craft.

Prior to my arrival, the office manager was Dr. Sam's wife, by default. She is one of the kindest, sweetest individuals you will ever meet. She will literally do anything for anyone and especially Dr. Sams or me. The staff knew this and preyed upon her good nature like a group of siblings trying to convince their mother for some additional dessert. And like most moms, our office manager would more-times-than-not say "yes."

This led to a very relaxed environment, which if you are not in the healthcare field, may not seem like a bad thing, but when you couple a relaxed environment with no real management structure, you get what we had—CHAOS.

Now I'm not saying that everyone should be micromanaged, but there needs to be a happy medium. And in our clinic, there was no middle ground, it was either all or nothing. This is where the "self-management" comes into play that I alluded to earlier.

The staff knew that our office manager struggled with saying "no," so they would constantly come to her with requests, whether it be for time off, additional hours, or anything else they could think of. Like I said, she would more often than not say "yes," so then they quit asking and just started doing.

Here is a quick list of things that happened... again, NOT MAKING THIS UP.

Because the PT (who billed us by the hour) lived far away, she would often come in on the weekends to use the computers, office supplies, copiers, and postage for her direct marketing cosmetic business. After auditing this, I wonder how many years we funded this business?

The PT had busy kids who would often be in the office, playing on the gym equipment, or lounging in the office waiting on their mom. I am never productive when my kids are around.

The PTA had a baby. Because the PTA was really loved, she was allowed to bring the baby to work with her. Tricia kept a pack-n-play in her office and handled the baby while doing billing. The PTA had another baby and this time the baby would hang out in the PT gym. Often, the PTA would be treating a patient while the PT (who billed out at a much higher rate) would be holding the baby. That's an expensive baby-sitter. Because this PTA was actually dedicated to her job, she would put the patient experience above the baby's needs. One time I walked into the office, before I worked there, and there was a patient changing the baby's dirty diaper because she was tired of hearing the baby cry and smelling the stink.

Because they didn't have a good accounting system nor timeclocks, people would just fill out a paper timesheet. Every time the PT was gone, she would write "vacation" on her timesheet. Since this wasn't being tracked... let's just say she got paid for A LOT of vacation time.

The PT department did not want people to do the scheduling for them. So even though we had software that allowed the front desk to schedule, the PT department would literally YELL at the staff if any appointments were booked by anyone other than themselves. The staff became FEARFUL because of how snippy this department got about scheduling. Even the owners felt like they couldn't schedule a new patient without clearing it with their own employees.

Because of some of the above issues, it wasn't uncommon that the PT would have to come in on the weekends to finish her notes. This was on the clock, of course.

As time and familiarity continued, we noticed that even though a patient might be on the schedule for 45 minutes, we would only get a fee slip for a single unit of exercise (15-minute procedure) and then an E-stim (unattended modality). After a post-departure audit, we determined a sizable amount of under coding.

Ultimately, here was the problem. These people lost their passion. They were incredible therapists at one time. I don't know what happened, but they were great. They stopped being great. Don't kid yourself; your patients can feel and see when you lose your passion.

Remember that first meal I had on my first day on the job? It was with this department! Go figure!

I believe in reconciliation. I tried hard over the next couple of months to get this department going with the people I had. EVERYTHING I would implement, they would shoot down. They didn't feel the need to grow. They didn't feel the need to change. Fortunately for me, they both quickly decided that they needed to "explore new opportunities."

I'm sure that after their resignations (within 2 weeks of each other) I had to have another "Tsunami" conversation with Trish. The PT had been with them for 11 ½ years! She was really all they knew and now the new guy has run them both off in what once was a thriving practice.

After they left, I did a financial audit of the department. I determined that the department had made just at $147 that year. Yes, you read that correctly, ONE HUNDRED FORTY-SEVEN DOLLARS. After doing this audit, I pulled Dr. Sams aside and told him he made $147 from the PT department. He questioned me on the amount. I confirmed for him that it was a TOTAL of $147 for the past 10 months. His words: "I've put up with that for only $147?"

What are you putting up with for "only $147?"

ACTION STEPS:

What areas are your staff taking advantage of you, your management, or your nature?

What areas are you NOT managing your company correctly?

What is your staff devoting their time to while in your office/on your timeclock?

Are there members of your staff (or yourself) who have lost their passion?

What are you putting up with for "only $147?"

If you can identify any of these areas in your own business, take the necessary steps to change the direction of your company. If not, be thankful that you have a great team in place that is working hard to make your dream a success!

CHAPTER 8

Slow to Hire and Fast to Fire

I remember before I was married, I was working out in the yard with my dad and I asked him if Jaime was the girl I was supposed to marry. He gave me some of the most profound advice I have ever received that can be used in marriage AND business. He said, "The only thing worse than no wife, is the wrong wife. Choose Wisely!" What amazing advice. All you have to do is replace the word wife with almost anything. The only thing worse than no employees, is the wrong employees!

Basically, I'm putting this chapter in here because we all love it when someone else has been as miserable (or more so) as us.

If you want to skip these stories, here is what I want you to learn. You can't afford to NOT hire the right people. That might mean firing some people that aren't keeping up with your core values.

Now, on to our stories.

- I told you about the PTA who brought the babies into the office. What I didn't tell you was that I had to "FIRE THE BABY." I gave the baby a 2-week notice and told her mom that she couldn't come in to work anymore. My family still reminds me that I fired a baby one time!

• We had a doctor one time who (unbeknownst to us) was selling pharmaceuticals out of his trunk and was under full FBI investigation. The FBI agent called us and said we had two choices: fire him or go down with him since he was our employee. He was gone in less than 5 minutes.

• As I was cleaning up things with my front office staff, I had two employees try to leverage against me in a case of "She said, she said." Employee #1 came down to my office to tell me what Employee #2 was doing. I knew for a fact that Employee #1 was accurate in her assessment. I immediately called Employee #2 to come to my office so she and Employee #1 could hash it out right there. I gave Employee #2 the chance to tell her side of the story and caught her in a lie. I told her that we didn't allow lying. She said, "Oh God, is that how it's going to be?"

I said, "You mean that we will require employees to be honest?"

She said, "If that's how it is going to be, then I quit." I walked her to her car.

• We had a front desk lady who wanted to be a singer and she would just quietly hum all day long at work. She was a personable woman who had a daughterly-like demeanor with many of the patients. She was a single mother of four kids who basically had full-time custody. She didn't leave on the best of terms and was fired. She left the building pitching a potpourri of profanity, but that isn't the actual problem(s) that we discovered after she left. When she wasn't there on Monday, many of the patients were awkwardly irritated at us for her being gone. This happened for a couple of days. After further investigation, she had been "comping" many patients for their cash-based services.

BUT WAIT, THERE'S MORE! Like a missionary coming to raise monthly support, she had convinced SEVERAL of the patients that our company was unable to pay her enough to support her family so at least six patients (that we know of) were giving her a monthly support check to "feed her family!"

- Prior to my arrival, the office had a sneaky closet alcoholic who, after her departure, they found "brown bags" of alcohol bottles in various hiding places all over the office.

- I interviewed a delightful lady who claimed to have great computer skills. When put to the test, it was like watching a sloth use a mouse. On top of that, she had a tremor. She didn't make it very far in the vetting process. These are some pretty big red flags for a job that advertised "computer skills a must."

- I had a woman who worked for us for one day. She interviewed well via video (during COVID) and was well experienced. I asked her to start 2 days later. She contacted me the morning of her first day and she profusely apologized because her car was broken down. She said she would for sure be there the next day. The next day came and she was moving funny. She said her husband broke her ribs and laughed about it. She said he was having a bad dream and acted out in his sleep. We offered to x-ray her and help her out that morning, but she declined. As the day progressed, she started shaking while working (claiming it was her blood sugar). She went into the bathroom a couple of times and when she came out, she wouldn't be shaking for a while. At the end of the day, her husband came and picked her up. They left her car at the office. She didn't return the next day. Someone picked up her car overnight. We always wondered what was up with her and we always thought that rib story was bizarre. A few months later, I saw on the news that she had been murdered and her husband had been arrested as the primary suspect. Very sad ending to a very short employment.

• We had an employee one time who wouldn't put down his Rubik's Cube during patient care. I finally got him to stop doing it around patients, but in his off time, he would sit in the break room and time himself. He was super-fast and it was fun to watch, but it was annoying to listen to... ALL. THE. TIME.

• We had a male employee who would always let his clothes sour in the washing machine. We had to offer to do his work laundry, but he claimed he didn't need it. I took him out for a soda during a break and told him, "You stink and people are complaining." Fortunately, he took it to heart and corrected the issue.

• There is a product called Poo-Pourri. It is an amazing "spray before you go" toilet spray. The best way for it to work, is to actually use it and not leave it in the bottle. We had a guy who had such gut-rot issues, that he would use the employee bathroom and clear out the building with his stench. Patients would be in exam rooms and you would hear them say, "What is that?" "Did something die?" "What happened?" It wasn't good at all!

• We had another employee who had a side hustle that she didn't think we knew about. She would often have "stomach troubles" and end up being in the bathroom for a long time. What she didn't realize is the employee bathroom wasn't the best at keeping the sound out. She would be in there talking on the phone working her other business.

• We had an associate chiropractor who didn't want to make any money. This was weird since her entire pay was based upon collections. She would sit in her office with no patients nor the drive to get any more.

- We had another associate chiropractor who was an A.K. provider. We are not a high-volume clinic, but in 15-minute slots, a full day could easily be 30 patients. Anything over 16 visits was "too much" for him. One day, a new couple came in to see him. They were elderly. He was muscle testing the husband and the wife kept talking and nay-saying what he was doing. He throws open his door and yells "Damnit Maurice, you are blocking my energy here." He then yelled for me to come deal with them since Maurice wasn't letting him treat her husband like he wanted to.

- We had a nurse practitioner that when anything would go wrong with a patient (pass out, high blood pressure, nausea, pretty much anything that wasn't "normal"), she would come running out of her office yelling "OH GOD, Dr. Sams." We still yell this among the few remaining staff that remember her "Oh God..." calls.

- We had a PT one time who sat down with our patients and told them everything we did wrong as a company and how she would do it better. She wasn't with us that long.

- We had a female doctor who would wear sheer tops with fluorescent bras, or low cut tops with patterned bras. I had an elderly female patient pull me aside to complain, "I think she is trying to show my husband her breasts. I'm not sure why because she doesn't have anything to show, but it makes me uncomfortable." It is for reasons like this that my policy manual has a line in it that says something like, "The staff nor patients need to know what color of undergarment(s) you are wearing."

- Lastly, and most recently, I hired a Physical Therapist who no longer wanted to live in the state of California so he just started randomly applying for jobs anywhere not in California. He and I met in person and then over the next several months talked on the phone and communicated about him moving to Branson to take over a clinic I was purchasing with the full intent of him running it. He wasn't there a week until I realized that he wasn't a good fit for our company. It wasn't another week until he was no longer in our employ.

Around my 36-month mark at the company, we had gone through at least 40 employees. My daughter loves to ask me about it every day, "Do the same people who started the day still work for you this evening?" I have to remind her that we currently have a great team and this isn't something we still have to deal with… for now.

Why do I tell you all these stories? Obviously, you have read them and already judged our company and management style based upon very little data—only the data I have chosen to tell you. What I will tell you is that the majority of those people looked good on paper, interviewed well, and even passed a pretty strenuous vetting process. Some of them were long-time employees. Some didn't make it the first day. As you noticed, many of them were doctoral or provider level. **YOU CANNOT BE AFRAID** to terminate a person who is not good for your company—someone who goes against the culture of your company.

Remember: The only thing worse than no employee, is the wrong employee.

I made it a personal policy a long time ago that if I don't want to go to work because I don't want to be with another co-worker, then one of us has to leave. As the boss, the person leaving ISN'T going to be me!

ACTION STEPS:

Do I have some employees that are not representing my company well?

Can this be remedied?

Do they just need to be let go?

If you have employees that are not upholding the standards of your company, it may be time to let them go. This is especially true if they are not representing your company well. Employees that do not represent your company well can give off a negative image to potential customers and clients, which can ultimately hurt your business. If you have tried to remediate the situation and it has not worked, then letting the employee go may be the best course of action.

When you are interviewing potential employees, pay attention to red flags that may come up. If an applicant seems dishonest or unqualified, it may be best to move on to someone else. It is better to spend extra time looking for the right employees than to have to deal with the consequences of hiring the wrong ones.

If you do find yourself in a situation where you need to let an employee go, make sure to do it in a professional and respectful way. Give them a chance to explain their side of the story and let them know what they could have done differently. Thank them for their time and wish them the best in their future endeavors.

CHAPTER 9

Charge What You are Worth

As a society, we have been conditioned to believe that chiropractors are not "real" doctors. This couldn't be further from the truth! Chiropractors are highly trained and licensed professionals who provide an invaluable service to the community. As a profession, physical therapists have started shooting themselves in the foot with billing issues and declining reimbursements. Many independent doctors not in the hospital system are being viewed as outcasts.

Unfortunately, many chiropractors, PTs, and independent doctors do not charge what they are worth. In fact, many of them are undercharging for their services. This is likely due to the fact that chiropractors are not as well recognized or respected as other medical professionals, PTs are a disorganized profession, and the hospital systems are making independent doctors look like outcasts. As a result, they may feel that they have to charge less in order to compete with other providers.

When looking at the prices charged by chiropractors in the United States, the average cost per visit is $65. However, there is a wide range in what chiropractors charge, with some charging as little as $30 per visit and others charging over $200. The prices charged by physical therapists in the United States are also all over the place, with the average cost per visit being $85. However, there is a wide range in what PTs charge, with some charging as little as $50 per visit and others charging over $200.

Independent doctors are usually the ones getting squeezed by hospitals. Hospitals are able to reimburse less for the same services because they have more negotiating power. As a result, many independent doctors are trying to compete on price and are charging less than they should.

There are a number of factors that can affect the cost of an office visit. The type of insurance you have, the location of the office, the type of treatment being provided, and the length of the appointment can all play a role in the price.

In addition to the cost per visit, many chiropractors also offer additional services such as massage, acupuncture, and nutritional counseling. These services can add significant value to your overall health and well-being. Another service many offices offer is spinal decompression. My research shows that the average cost per visit for spinal decompression is $85.

Physical therapists can have add-on services like aquatic therapy, electrical stimulation, and ultrasound. These services can also add significant value to your overall health and well-being.

Medical doctors have the greatest flexibility to add on services ranging from physicals to EKGs, from Botox to X-Rays and MRIs. These services can also add significant value to your practice.

A new area that our office has gotten into recently is what the industry calls "niches." These are specific treatments and modalities that are higher ticket items that not all offices provide. One example of a niche service is Cold Laser Therapy. Other niche services are Functional Medicine, Decompression, Red Light Therapy, Weight Loss, Neuropathy, Gut Health, Erectile Dysfunction, PRP, and more. If your office does not offer any niche services, I would highly recommend looking into them. Not only do they provide additional income for your office, but they also set you apart from the competition.

About a year and a half ago, we added hormone pellet therapy to our services and have seen a sizeable increase of revenue and profit from this niche. The company we chose to go with for this service is called bioTE.

When it comes to pricing, my advice would be, not to be the lowest provider in the area. Not only does this devalue the services you provide, but it also attracts a lower quality clientele. You want to be known as the provider who gets results, not the provider who is the cheapest.

If you are currently undercharging for your services, I would encourage you to raise your prices. Your clients will be willing to pay more if they see the value in what you do. If you are not sure how to raise your prices, there are a number of resources available to help you. Remember that you are worth what someone is willing to pay for your services. Do not sell yourself short!

Another issue that I see in my office is underbilling or undercoding. Because you may like the patient, you feel bad for them so you mark down your services a level or two. This isn't right to do. Underbilling and undercharging is just as bad as overbilling. You are providing a valuable service and you deserve to be paid for it!

The insurance companies frown on underbilling and will often times audit your office if they see a pattern of it. Not only that, but it is unethical to provide a service and then not bill for it. If you are caught underbilling, you could be subject to legal action just like you can for overbilling. In fact, I have heard of chiropractors who have had their license suspended for underbilling!

So, to sum it up, make sure you are billing for all the services you provide and that you are charging what your services are worth. Your clients will be happy to pay a fair price for quality care, and you will be able to sleep well at night knowing you are running an ethical and profitable business.

ACTION STEPS:

What are you charging for your services?

> Each service.

> Do you even know?

How does what you charge compare with your area/region?

Are you the cheapest provider in town?

Is that your business strategy?

Can you raise your rates?

How much money would you make additionally per year?

What exactly are you selling?

> Your time?

> Skills?

> Information?

> All of the above?

Can you package what you offer in a different way to increase perceived value and thus your rates?

Are you providing any niche services that command higher prices?

What is the quality of your clients?

CHAPTER 10

Nutrition and Practice Growth

Americans spend a staggering $32 billion a year on 85,000 different vitamins, minerals, and other nutritional supplements. Overall, Americans will spend $21 billion on vitamins and herbal supplements in 2015. Last year, Americans spent nearly $50 billion on vitamins and supplements.

What's more, $30.2 billion is spread out among 59 million Americans, meaning the average person who buys supplements spends over $500 a year on them. Americans spend an average of $2.1 billion annually on weight loss supplements. Older Americans spend more on supplements than younger Americans.

As ever, nutritional supplements are becoming a staple in many American households. By 2022, at least 77% of Americans are taking at least one nutritional supplement, and the percentage is even higher among older adults. The use of multiple nutritional supplements (two, three, four, or more) increased with age; nearly a quarter of adults 60 and older (24.9%) reported taking one or more nutritional supplements.

Because the nutrition and supplement portion of many practices is overlooked, I'm going to quickly go over what these vitamins and supplements are and their most common purpose.

Multivitamins- Multivitamins are the most popular type of supplement, taken by more than one-third of Americans. They are typically taken to improve overall health or to prevent vitamin deficiencies.

Vitamin D- Vitamin D is the second most popular type of supplement, taken by more than one-fourth of Americans. It is often taken to improve bone health and prevent osteoporosis.

Omega-3 fatty acids- Omega-3 fatty acids are found in fish oil supplements and are taken for a variety of reasons, including heart health, brain health, and joint pain relief.

Probiotics- Probiotics are live microorganisms that are similar to the beneficial bacteria found in the gut. They are often taken to improve digestive health and boost the immune system.

Calcium- Calcium is a mineral that is essential for bone health. It is often taken as a supplement to prevent osteoporosis or to treat calcium deficiency.

Vitamin C- Vitamin C is an antioxidant that plays a role in many body processes, including the formation of collagen and the absorption of iron. It is often taken to improve immunity or to prevent colds and other infections.

Protein powders- Protein powders are dietary supplements that contain concentrated sources of protein, such as whey or casein. They are often taken by bodybuilders and other athletes to improve muscle mass and strength.

Iron- Iron is a mineral that is needed for the production of hemoglobin, a protein that carries oxygen in the blood. It is often taken as a supplement to treat iron deficiency or anemia.

B vitamins- B vitamins are a group of water-soluble vitamins that play important roles in energy metabolism and the synthesis of red blood cells. They are often taken to improve energy levels or to prevent vitamin deficiencies.

Magnesium- Magnesium is a mineral that is involved in many body processes, including muscle contraction, nerve function, and blood sugar regulation. It is often taken to treat migraines, restless leg syndrome, and type 2 diabetes.

If protein powders are included, the market for supplements is as large as all organic products combined. About 1,000 new supplements enter the market each year. Supplements can be very expensive, as evidenced by the $50 billion Americans spend each year on various forms, and that number is rising every year.

So I guess my follow-up question to you, the practice owner, would be this: Is any of that $50 billion making it to your bottom line each year?

There are some quality supplement manufacturers out there, I will include a non-comprehensive list in the action steps below.

Most supplements are marked up 100% (or doubled) of what you pay for them. We keep a sizeable amount of inventory at our office, but we also do a large amount of sales annually in supplements alone.

I went into an obstetrician's office one time with my wife when she was pregnant and I noticed that they sold no supplements. I spoke to the practice manager about selling supplements and he said it wasn't worth his time. Let me break that down for you real quickly.

If an OB office would only sell quality prenatal vitamins and educate their patients on the importance of QUALITY supplements here's what just a single item could do to their bottom line: If you have 100 patients a year and you convince ½ of them to take these supplements. (This may seem a high percentage, but we are talking about babies here.) They take the prenatals for the 9 months of their pregnancy, plus an additional 6 months while exclusively breastfeeding (most offer breastmilk longer, though not exclusively). This is 15 boxes of prenatal vitamins that they could sell per person. So 50 people times 15 boxes is 750 total boxes sold annually. The prenatal I was referring to has a profit of $30 per box. That is an annual PROFIT of $22,500.

To put that profit in perspective, considering a full-time employee works approximately 2080 hours per year, that profit alone could pay for $10.82/hr of that person's wages... by only adding a single supplement.

Before I close this down, if you are going to add supplements and you know nothing about them, I encourage you to educate yourself on the supplements that you are going to sell. Many of the manufacturers offer classes, some of them even have CEU credit. Important: You can mess someone up by giving them the wrong or poor quality supplements.

ACTION STEPS:

Here are some supplement companies that you can sell in your office:

    Orthomolecular – https://www.orthomolecularproducts.com
    Nordic Naturals – https://www.nordicnaturals.com/en
    Standard Process – https://www.standardprocess.com/
    Metagenics – https://www.metagenics.com/
    Barlow Herbal – https://barlowherbal.com/
    Xymogen – https://www.xymogen.com/
    Pure Encapsulations – https://www.pureencapsulations.com/

Professional Complementary Formulas – https://professionalformulas.com/
Bach Remedies – https://www.bachflower.com/
Douglas Laboratories – https://www.douglaslabs.com/
Designs for Health – https://www.designsforhealth.com/

There are many supplement companies out there, but not all of them provide quality products. When you are choosing a company to partner with, look for one that offers classes and education on their products, so that you can be sure you are selling the right supplements to your patients.

This is in no way a comprehensive list. If I can give you further advice on this, my contact info is in the last chapter.

If you are going to do many supplements, I encourage you to streamline the checkout process by using a point-of-sale system. In this industry, you get what you pay for. I have settled on an online company called "HIKE." They accomplish most of what I need for a point-of-sale system. You can find them at www.hikeup.com

CHAPTER 11

Marketing and Social Media

IF YOU BUILD IT, THEY WON'T JUST COME.

Though entire books could be and have been devoted to this topic, I wanted to put it on your radar if it isn't already. When our practice opened 23 years ago, it slowly built momentum and word-of-mouth took over. The ONLY advertising we did for years was a yellow-page ad and a weekly radio show. We didn't need to advertise. However, those days are long gone. Unlike Kevin Costner in the movie *Field of Dreams*, if you build it, they won't just come!

Though the industry will tell you that 11% is acceptable to spend on marketing, that freaks many of you out because you haven't ever spent much money on marketing. In this chapter, I'm going to briefly go over some things we have done to gain new patients. This list is not comprehensive, but maybe it will give you some food for thought as you think about scaling your practice.

Let's start with the easy ones. I call this Low Lying Fruit or basic marketing.

How long have you been in practice? Do you have a database? They say that a database is one of your greatest assets. You can leverage your database for marketing by doing the following:

1. First, make sure every patient that comes in the door is in your database. This seems like a no-brainer, but you would be surprised how many times I go into practices and they don't have everyone in their database or they don't have accurate text numbers and email addresses.

2. If you have been in practice for a while, do you have a system for PURGING your database of people who haven't been in to see you in years? You want to keep your database clean so that when you do mailings and such, you aren't wasting money on postage. You also don't want to place a phone call to remind a deceased person about your services.

3. Do you have a system for STAYING IN TOUCH with your database on a regular basis? You can do this via postcards, letters, emails, or even texts.

4. Do you have an automated system in place for BIRTHDAYS and ANNIVERSARIES? This is a great way to stay in touch and make your patients feel special.

5. Do you have a system for FOLLOWING UP with new patients? You want to make sure that you are staying in touch with them so they don't forget about you and go back to their old doctor.

6. Do you have a system for REFERRALS? Asking your patients for referrals is one of the best ways to grow your practice.

7. Do you have a system for TESTIMONIALS? Asking your patients for testimonials is a great way to show new patients that you are the real deal. We talk about this in our chapter about Google Reviews.

8. Do you have a system for SOCIAL MEDIA? This is one of the best ways to reach new patients. Make sure you are active on all of the major social media platforms.

This is just the tip of the iceberg when it comes to marketing, but if you aren't doing these things, you are missing out on easy ways to grow your practice.

Next, we will discuss some more advanced marketing strategies. I call this section ADVANCED MARKETING.

1. One of the best ways to reach new patients is through SEO or search engine optimization. This is the process of making your website show up higher in Google when people search for keywords related to what you do. For example, if someone searches for "physical therapy in Colorado Springs" you want your website to show up on the first page of Google. If you aren't on the first page, you might as well not be on Google at all. Studies have shown that people almost NEVER go to the second page of Google when they are looking for something.

2. Another great way to reach new patients is through Google AdWords. This is the process of paying Google to have your ad show up at the top of the page when people search for keywords related to what you do. For example, if someone searches for "physical therapy in Colorado Springs" you can pay Google to have your ad show up at the top of the page. People will then click on your ad and be taken to your website.

3. Another great way to reach new patients is through Facebook Ads. Facebook Ads are a great way to target potential patients who might not be aware of your practice. For example, you can target people who live in Colorado Springs, who are over the age of 18, and who have an interest in physical therapy. Then you can show them an ad for your practice. Facebook Ads are very effective and can be very inexpensive if done correctly.

4. Another great way to reach new patients is through print advertising. This can be a great way to reach people who might not be aware of your practice. For example, you can place an ad in the phone book, above a urinal, or in a local magazine. Print advertising can be very effective if done correctly.

5. Another great way to reach new patients is through direct mail. This is a great way to target potential patients who might not be aware of your practice. For example, you can send out postcards or flyers to people in Colorado Springs. Direct mail can be very effective if done correctly. The USPS has a great product called EDDM (Every Door Direct Mail) where you can pick a specific neighborhood or mail route to send direct mail to. When we send invites to events, we hire some Jr. High girls to hand-write our envelopes and we put the invite in a colored greeting card envelope. They say that this will get up at a 92% open rate!

6. Another great way to reach new patients is through word of mouth. This is the best way to reach new patients. For example, if you have a satisfied patient, ask them to tell their friends and family about your practice. Word of mouth is the best form of advertising.

7. Another great way to reach new patients is through referral programs. This is a great way to get people to refer their friends and family to your practice. For example, you can offer a discount to people who refer their friends and family to your practice. Referral programs are a great way to get people to spread the word about your practice. There are some laws about this, so be careful on this one.

8. Another great way to reach new patients is through community outreach. This is a great way to get involved in the community and to let people know about your practice. For example, you can participate in health fairs, give talks at local schools, or sponsor a little league team. Community outreach is a great way to get your name out there and to let people know about your practice. We call numbers at the senior center for BINGO.

9. Another great way to reach new patients is through online directories. This is a great way to get your practice listed in online directories. For example, you can list your practice in Google Places, Yelp, and Angie's List. Online directories are a great way to get your practice seen by potential patients.

10. Another great way to reach new patients is through social media. This is a great way to connect with potential patients and to let them know about your practice. For example, you can create a Facebook or Instagram page for your practice and post updates about your practice. You can also use Twitter to tweet about your practice. Record some videos for TikTok. Social media is a great way to connect with potential patients and to let them know about your practice.

11. I cannot emphasize enough the importance of online reviews. We have laminated QR codes in each of the exam rooms and the front desk. We train our staff on soliciting them.

12. Another great way to reach new patients is through blog posts. This is a great way to share information about your practice with potential patients. For example, you can write blog posts about the services you offer, the staff at your practice, or the community you serve. Blog posts are a great way to share information about your practice with potential patients, especially through social channels.

13. We created waiting room videos that feature our staff and doctors. This was a great way to introduce potential patients to our practice and services in a non-threatening way. The first month I put my television up in the lobby, we generated over $4,000 in sales for a specific product.

14. I have been on a couple of television programs telling about our practice. Sometimes this is organic and sometimes this is paid.

Mark being interviewed on a syndicated health program

15. The last one I want to throw out there is Screenings or Total Body Assessments. These have been a gold mine for us. They are especially well received when we give out free t-shirts for the "first 15 people" who sign up.

Maybe these will give you some ideas on how to market your practice or maybe these will just remind you that you are already doing the right things.

My last piece of advice on this topic is try to make sure you can "track" your ad spend. Then you will know if what you spent on it was worth your time, energy, and effort.

ACTION STEPS:

Do you have a marketing strategy?

Do you have a marketing budget?

What are some ways in which you want to market your practice in the coming year?

CHAPTER 12

Clean Up Your Practice

When my wife was a kid, she used to go to a dentist in town who had a hornet's nest hanging from the ceiling as decoration. Yes, a literal hornet's nest. I always thought it was weird until I started going into other people's offices. Though you might not have a hornet's nest, what does the appearance of your office portray about the type of practice you run?

ACTION STEPS:

Literally walk around your office with a notepad and analyze the various parts of each room/element:

EXTERIOR:

> Is it clean?

> Are the windows washed?

> Inside and out?

> Are there hazards?

Is it easy for people to get in and out?

Is it easy for people to know where to go and what to do via signage (if necessary)?

Is there adequate parking?

Is there handicapped parking?

INTERIOR:

How does it smell? Fresh? Stuffy? Moldy?

> (you are probably nose blind to this... ask someone who has never been there before)

What is the condition of the flooring?

Is it clean?

Does it have a bunch of gross spots (if carpet)?

Is it cluttered?

WAITING ROOM:

Do you have comfortable chairs?

Do you have chairs that larger people can fit in?

Is it cluttered?

What is the age of your waiting room reading material?

> What is the condition of it?

Do you have something for them to drink?

Is there a trashcan available?

If you have toys in your waiting room:

Are they clean and easy to sanitize?

Are they in disrepair?

TOILETS:

Do you have appropriate waste dispensers suitable for your menstruating female patients?

Does it smell bad in there?

Do you need to provide a product like Poo-pourri?

Do you have easy to use hand towels?

Do you have soap?

Are your trashcans making the room look cluttered?

Is it cleaned often?

TREATMENT ROOMS:

Are they cluttered?

Do you have updated things on the walls?

Or are they the same things that were there 20 years ago?

Do you have piles of things that you NEVER use anymore?

What is the condition of your treatment tables?

Is the vinyl/leather ripped or cracked?

Do you have appropriate disposal containers?

Sharps, trash, etc.

Is your equipment properly working?

GYM:

Is it cluttered?

Do you have pieces of broken equipment?

Do you have ancient pieces that would scare someone by looking at it?

What is the condition of your mats, etc.?

ASK YOURSELF:

What needs repaired?

What needs cleaned?

WHAT DO MY PATIENTS SEE WHEN THEY COME IN?

CHAPTER 13

Ring Ring... Hello

The ability to properly answer a phone is a dying art. Though even senior citizens are texting, you can't neglect that calm and caring voice on the other end of the phone asking if they can help.

In today's age of technology, it's easy to forget the importance of good old-fashioned telephone etiquette—especially in a doctor's office. First impressions are important, and the way you greet a patient on the phone can set the tone for their entire visit.

Unfortunately, poor telephone etiquette is becoming more and more common in doctor's offices. A study by Harris Interactive found that 62% of consumers have hung up the phone out of frustration due to poor customer service. This is not only bad for business, but it can also lead to patients taking their business elsewhere. In fact, 86% of consumers said they would be willing to pay more for a better customer service experience.

It's time to put an end to this problem by providing your staff with the resources they need to deliver excellent telephone service. In this chapter, we'll talk about why good telephone etiquette is important, common mistakes that are made, and how you can fix them.

WHY GOOD TELEPHONE ETIQUETTE IS IMPORTANT

As we mentioned before, first impressions are important. When a patient calls your office, they are looking for help—and it's your job to make sure they get the assistance they need as quickly and efficiently as possible. If the person who answers the phone is rude or unprofessional, it will reflect poorly on your practice as a whole and may discourage patients from seeking treatment.

Think about it this way—would you want to do business with someone who was rude to you on the phone? Probably not. The same goes for your patients. I remember several receptionists who were at our office in the years prior to my arrival on staff. There are two in particular who were downright mean. In fact, one of them was one of my first "relocations" after taking the job as Chief of Staff.

In addition to creating a bad impression, poor telephone etiquette can also lead to lost business. As we mentioned before, Harris Interactive found that 62% of consumers have hung up the phone out of frustration due to poor customer service. This number is even higher for younger generations—78% of millennials say they've hung up the phone out of frustration. If your staff isn't providing excellent customer service, there's a good chance you're losing business to one of your competitors who is.

So now that we've talked about why good telephone etiquette is important, let's take a look at some common mistakes that are made and how you can fix them...

COMMON MISTAKES THAT ARE MADE

One of the most common problems with telephone etiquette is putting people on hold without letting them know first. Patients hate being put on hold—and for good reason. According to Forbes Insights, 64% of customers say being put on hold is their number one pet peeve when speaking with businesses over the phone. Not only is being put on hold frustrating, but it also makes people feel like they're not a priority. If you absolutely must put someone on hold (for example, if you need to ask another staff member for help), be sure to let them know first so they don't feel like they're being ignored. You might say something like, "I'm just going to put you on hold for one minute while I grab that information for you." By doing this, you'll avoid frustrating your patients and maintain a positive relationship with them.

Another mistake that's often made is forgetting basic manners such as saying "please" and "thank you". These may seem like small things, but they can make a big difference in the way your patients perceive your staff. According to a study conducted by American Express, 61% of consumers say they're more likely to do business with companies that are polite. So if you want to keep your patients happy (and attract new ones), be sure your staff is using basic manners when speaking on the phone.

Finally, another common mistake that's made is putting patients through a lengthy telephone menu before they're able to speak with a live person. According to the same study by American Express, 67% of consumers say they've hung up the phone out of frustration because they had to listen to a long menu of options. If your patients are forced to listen to a long list of options before they're able to speak with a live person, there's a good chance they'll get frustrated and take their business elsewhere.

HOW TO MAKE A GOOD IMPRESSION

There are some simple things your receptionist can do to make sure every call is handled professionally. Here are a few suggestions:

- Answer the phone within three rings.
- Use a pleasant and professional tone of voice.

- Research has shown that smiling while on the phone can be perceived by people on the other end.
- Speak slowly and clearly.
- Greet the caller by name if possible.
- Take time to listen to the patient's concerns.
- Never put a caller on hold without asking first.
- Follow up with patients after appointments to make sure they had a good experience.

I have a "script" for my staff to use when answering the phone: "Healing Arts Center, this is ____________, how may I help you." I have noticed recently there is a shift in that type of statement from "How may I help you" to "I can help you" which indicates the receptionist is empowered to assist the caller.

ACTION STEPS:

Have a trusted friend that your office doesn't know do a "secret shopper" call in to your office and have them give you an honest opinion of your phone process.

Does your staff know how you want them to answer the phone?

Are they consistent in this?

Do they smile when they answer the phone?

Are they empowered with knowledge to keep things off of your plate?

Make sure your staff knows it is okay to take a message for any of the doctors or providers in the office, rather than trying to direct the call themselves.

If you have an automated phone system, make sure it is not too long and that it gives your patients the option to speak to a live person.

Finally, make sure you are following up with patients after their appointments to get feedback on their overall experience in your office. This is a great way to catch any small problems before they turn into bigger ones.

CHAPTER 14

I'm Not in Sales

If you ask most doctors whether they see themselves as salespeople, the answer is likely to be a resounding "no." And yet, in many ways, doctors are constantly having to sell their patients on various treatment options, whether it's convincing them to take a certain medication/supplement or having a particular procedure done.

Of course, there's a big difference between selling a patient something they need and simply pushing unnecessary treatments or products. But at the end of the day, doctors are often in the business of convincing people to do things that may be in their best interest—and that's not an easy task.

It takes a lot of skill to be able to effectively sell someone on a treatment plan. You have to be able to understand their needs and concerns, build trust, and ultimately show them that you have their best interests at heart. And while it may not be something that most doctors like to think about, the reality is that sales skills are essential in many aspects of medicine.

I have yet to meet a doctor that said they received the proper "sales" training in college and above. The good news is that there are many sales books, articles, and resources available to help doctors brush up on their skills. If you're looking to improve your ability to sell patients on treatment plans, I highly recommend checking out some of those resources or reach out to us and we can get you going with some great coaches.

In the meantime, here are a few tips that may help:

1. Be transparent about your reasons for recommending a certain treatment.

Many patients are hesitant to take a doctor's recommendation at face value; they want to know why you're suggesting a particular course of action. So, it's important to be upfront about your reasoning. Explain the benefits of the treatment, as well as any risks or potential side effects. The more information you can provide, the better equipped the patients you will have. You also need to know any contrary information about your suggestions that is out there on "GOOGLE." Don't forget, these patients have their doctorate in Google!

2. Take the time to listen to your patients.

It's important to understand where your patients are coming from and what their needs and concerns are. Only then will you be able to address them in a way that will be convincing. So, take the time to really listen to what they have to say. And don't be afraid to ask questions if you're not sure about something.

3. Build trust with your patients.

If patients don't trust you, they're not going to be open to taking your advice, no matter how well reasoned it may be. So, it's important to build trust with your patients from the outset. This means being honest and transparent, as well as keeping your word. If you say you're going to do something, make sure you follow through.

4. Show that you have your patients' best interests at heart.

At the end of the day, patients want to know that you're looking out for their best interests and not just trying to make a quick buck. So, it's important to show that you care about your patients and their well-being. This may mean going above and beyond in terms of customer service or taking the time to really get to know your patients on a personal level.

5. Be Persistent.

It takes a lot of skill and practice to be a good salesperson, but it's worth it if it means being able to help your patients get the treatment they need. So, don't give up if you don't see results immediately. Keep working at it and honing your skills. And soon enough, you'll be a pro at convincing patients to take your recommendations.

6. The Art of Silence

This is a very important sales tip, but not one that is used enough. Remember, "He who talks first, loses." So, when you are making a recommendation to a patient, once you have given them the recommendation, stay quiet while they think it over.

7. Be Enthusiastic.

Patients want to see that you're passionate about what you're recommending. So, make sure you show enthusiasm when you're talking about a particular treatment or product. The more excited you are about it, the more likely patients will be to take your advice.

8. Use Testimonials

If you have any success stories of patients who have benefited from a particular service that you offer, use them.

I have always said that there are two great sales people in the medical community—the oncologist and the dentist. They both have mastered their craft so well to create urgency, build trust, and close the sale.

Oncologists are only second to the dental industry in sales. These people will make you wait 6 months for a visit and then need to "immediately" treat you with very expensive drugs that may or may not work. They have perfected their sales skills to get you to make a decision on the spot.

Some oncologists will use scare tactics while others will create a sense of urgency. Here are some examples:

1. "If we don't start treatment right away, the cancer will spread and it will be much harder to treat."

2. "This is your only chance at survival."

3. "The sooner we start treatment, the better your chances are of beating this."

4. "I've seen patients in your situation before and I know what works best."

5. "Trust me, I'm a doctor."

If only you could apply some of these same points to your current practice, you might have much less attrition and much greater patient retainage.

ACTION STEPS:

Do you consider yourself a sales person?

If you answered "NO" to the above question, please revisit this chapter and understand that if YOU (as the owner) aren't willing to "sell" his/her services, why would anyone else believe enough in your practice to do the same?

What is the hardest part about sales for you?

Conversation?

Asking for money?

Is this because you don't think you are worth what you are charging?

CHAPTER 15

Right Bus, Wrong Seat

When I was a youth pastor, I went to a conference that had breakout sessions that you could choose from. I never really liked those conferences, but I had to choose one, so I chose the one called "How to Fire a Volunteer." I was amazed at how much I learned from that class that I have been able to take with me from job to job.

One of the parts of the class was talking about people being on the right bus (your office), but in the wrong seat (their exact job). It's a picture that has always stuck with me.

I think we can all think of someone who is great at their job, but maybe not so great at others. Maybe they are really good at customer service, but not so good at sales. Or they are really good at accounting, but not so good at HR. Whatever the case may be, we all have our strengths and weaknesses.

The key is to put people in the right seat on the bus. If they are good at customer service, put them in a job where they are interacting with customers. If they are good at accounting, put them in a job where they are working with numbers

The beauty of this is two-fold. First, the person is much more likely to be successful in their job if they are doing what they are good at. Second, it frees up other people to do their jobs better.

So often, we have someone in a job that they are struggling with and it brings the whole team down. But if we can move them to a job that they are better suited for, it will not only help them, but it will help the whole team.

A problem we have had at our office before with this concept is the fact that many people lack self-awareness. This is a point I hammer home with my staff weekly. I remind them that it is okay to be aware of your faults, and that we always need to be honing our skills in life.

So, next time you are thinking about making a change in your office, think about who might be in the wrong seat on the bus. I have this very conversation with many staff members. With some, it goes well and is successful; with others, not so much. But ultimately, their departure might be the best for your clinic anyway. Remember: they weren't doing their job well enough to begin with or you wouldn't have made the suggestion.

While on the subject, I can't emphasize enough that sometimes you will see that you have amazing employees who just aren't the right fit for you OR your clinic. More than once, I have sat down with an employee and had the opposite "right seat, wrong bus" conversation. It's not an easy conversation to have, but it is so important.

I recently had to have this conversation with an employee who was an amazing customer service representative. But the thing was, she was amazing at customer service for a retail store, not a medical office. I sat down with her and explained that while I thought she was an amazing customer service representative, I didn't think she was the right fit for our office. I offered to help her find a job that would be a better fit for her strengths.

It's not always easy to have these conversations, but they are so important. If you have an employee who is struggling in their job, have the conversation with them. You might be surprised at how willing they are to change seats on the bus or how excited they are to get off the bus!

ACTION STEPS:

WRONG SEAT

What employees do you have that need a change of seat?

Do you have any seats to provide them?

If money and personnel were not a factor, what would you change with the personnel in your office?

WRONG BUS

What employees do you have that are on the wrong bus?

CHAPTER 16

Zone of Genius

KNOWING YOUR ZONE OF GENIUS AND STAYING IN YOUR LANE

I was in a wreck in 2015. This wasn't a normal wreck; it was a pretty major collision. So major, that I did 5 days of therapy a week for over a year. During this time, I consulted with Dr. Sams (the guy whose practice I am currently running) about problems and symptoms I was having as a result of this wreck. One time, my field of vision started to really narrow, so he made a hypothesis that my pituitary stalk had some damage which was causing pressure on the optic nerve. He then said, "Find the best SOT therapist in the Kansas City metro and go see them." When I asked him what to do if I couldn't find that therapist, he said, "Then I will go to class and learn." I love this about him, but as he has now admitted, we were much better off finding someone who was passionate about SOT and well learned.

As a doctor, you have a lot of knowledge. You know a lot about the human body and how to treat different ailments. But there is also a limit to what you know. And that's okay! It's actually good for your business to stay within your zone of genius. Here's why:

1. You Can't Be an Expert at Everything.

No matter how smart you are, you can't be an expert at everything. That's why it's important to focus on the things you're good at and leave the rest to other people who are better equipped to handle it. Not only will this make you better at your job, but it will also free up your time so that you can focus on other things.

2. You'll Be More Productive.

When you focus on the things you're good at, you'll be more productive. You'll be able to get more done in less time because you won't be wasting time trying to figure out things that are outside of your area of expertise. This will help you grow your business faster and make more money in the long run.

3. Your Patients Will Appreciate It.

Your patients will appreciate it when you refer them to someone who is better equipped to handle their specific problem. They'll know that you're not just trying to get rid of them and that you really care about their well-being. This will build trust between you and your patients and make them more likely to come back to you in the future.

4. Referral Sources

You can develop relationships with other doctors and referral sources. For example, if you are a physical therapist who is not good at manipulations, send the patient to a chiropractor who can help their skeleton while you continue to do the body/muscle work on them. This could be the beginning of a great referral relationship.

5. Focus on Marketing.

You could take the time you were spending trying to learn something you will never use again to focus on marketing and promoting the areas of medicine that you are good at. When you try to do everything, it is difficult to market yourself effectively because you are trying to promote too many things at once. However, when you focus on just a few areas, you can develop targeted marketing campaigns that will be more effective in promoting your business.

So, what does all this mean for you? It means that you should focus on the things you're good at and leave the rest to other people who are better equipped than you. It also means that referring patients to other doctors is not only acceptable, but it's actually beneficial for both you and your patients!

I don't know why chiropractors are some of the worst at this, but you are not admitting failure by not being able to do everything. Western Medicine figured this out years ago, that you don't have to be able to do everything to and for everyone. I remember my M.D. friend Dr. Bill Weatherford years ago telling me all the things he "could" do, and then the list of the things he didn't have to do anymore. It's liberating.

You are actually helping your patients by referring them to someone who can help them better. So, stay in your lane and focus on what you're good at! Your patients will thank you for it.

ACTION STEPS:

1. Make a list of the things you're good at.

2. Make a list of the things you're not so good at.

3. Focus on the things you're good at and delegate or refer out the rest.

4. Develop relationships with other doctors and referral sources.

5. Stay focused.

CHAPTER 17

Command Respect vs. Demand Respect

I heard a wise saying one time that said, "Where there is no vision, the people will perish." How true is that? Certain people are made to lead, while others are made to follow. Even a leader can follow another leader if there is vision and forethought into whatever the task at hand is. My dad used to say this, "If you think you are a leader, but no one is following you, you are just an idiot out taking a walk." I believe that there are a countless number of people out there who are longing for a leader. The first step to being this leader is gaining the respect of the people following you. Remember, you just need one!

There's a big difference between commanding respect and demanding respect. If you demand respect, people may comply with what you say, but they won't necessarily follow your lead. On the other hand, if you command respect, people will not only do what you say, but they'll also want to follow your lead.

So how do you go about commanding respect? It starts with having the right attitude and approach. You need to be confident without being cocky, sincere without being smarmy, and competent without being a know-it-all. In other words, you need to be humble. People are more likely to follow someone who is humble than someone who is full of themselves.

Another important quality of a leader is decisiveness. People need to know that you're in charge and that you can make decisions. If you hem and haw over every little decision, your employees will start to lose faith in you. That's not to say that you should never listen to input from others, but at the end of the day, someone has to make the call, and that someone should be you. Remember, you need to keep that football!

Finally, you need to be able to inspire people. This doesn't mean giving rah-rah speeches all the time (although those can be effective occasionally). It means being passionate about what you do and conveying that passion to others. When people see how much you believe in your vision, they'll be more likely to buy into it themselves.

Here are some practical ways to demonstrate leadership to where your employees will want to respect you.

- Be the one who is always learning. Leaders are readers. They are also students of people and situations. You will notice that the best leaders are also the ones who continue to learn.
- Lead by example in everything you do. This includes being on time, completing assignments, cooperating with co-workers, respecting others, and exhibiting a positive attitude.
- Create an environment that supports respect. This includes setting expectations for employees regarding their behavior and performance, providing feedback both positive and negative in a constructive manner, and maintaining consistent standards.
- Encourage employees to take responsibility for their actions. In other words, don't make excuses for them or try to protect them from the consequences of their mistakes. This doesn't mean that you should be harsh or unsympathetic, but employees need to know that they are ultimately responsible for their own actions.

- Employees know when you trust them. Give them responsibility and be there to assist, but not take over the job. There is a guy in the physical therapy world named Aaron Lebauer. He has a statement that says, "80% is good enough." I have heard it said before that if you delegate something to someone and they do it 80% as good as you, you need to let them keep that thing you delegated as they hone in those skills.
- Finally, show appreciation for employees who respect you and follow your lead. A simple "thank you" can go a long way toward inspiring others to do the same.

So remember, commanding respect is not about demanding compliance. It's about having the right attitude, being decisive, and inspiring others to follow your lead. Do those things, and you'll be well on your way to becoming a respected leader.

It can be difficult to tell if an employee does not respect you. Often, there are subtle clues that an employee is not respecting you as their boss. Here are the top 10 ways to tell if an employee does not respect you as the boss.

1. They are consistently late for meetings and appointments with you.

2. They cancel or reschedule meetings with you at the last minute without a valid reason.

3. They avoid eye contact when speaking with you.

4. They openly disagree with your decisions or give criticism that is not constructive.

5. They gossip about you or complain about you to other employees.

6. They take credit for your ideas or try to take credit for the work of others.

7. They are constantly testing your authority by challenging your decisions or rules.

8. They do not listen when you are speaking or they interrupt you frequently.

9. They do not follow through on assignments or tasks that you have given them.

10. They do not show appreciation for your feedback or guidance.

If you notice any of these behaviors from an employee, it is likely that they do not respect you as their boss. It is important to try to address the issue early on so that it does not escalate and impact job performance or morale in the office.

ACTION STEPS:

Do you consider yourself a leader?

Is anyone following you?

Who are the leaders in your office?

Is anyone following them?

Are you respected by your employees?

Can you tell the difference if an employee respects you?

Do you show respect to others in your actions?

In your words?

CHAPTER 18

Hiring Professionals

Though I have dealt with some of these topics in other chapters, I feel that a short chapter on this topic is necessary, because these literally are the things that make or break a business, or get you thrown in jail.

Taxes, documents, and liability. These are just a few of the things that can cause headaches for doctors who own their own business. By hiring professionals to handle these things, you can free up your time to focus on what you do best: taking care of patients. Here's a look at a few ways hiring professionals can save you time and money.

OUTSOURCING YOUR ACCOUNTING

If you are still doing your taxes by yourself... seriously quit it. Do you like your patients performing some of your services on themselves? Not typically. The same is true with accounting. By outsourcing your accounting to a professional, you can free up your time to focus on more important things—like seeing patients. A professional accountant can also help you save money on taxes by taking advantage of deductions and credits that you may not be aware of. And if the IRS comes knocking, you'll have someone on your side who knows the ins and outs of the tax code and can help resolve any issues.

While on the topic of accountants, make sure the accountant is working for YOU and NOT for the IRS. When I first came to this office, they were telling me about all the taxes they were paying. I knew what they were grossing and I guessed at the expenses and it just made ZERO sense. I spent the next few months getting the books in order. They were in shambles. After we did that, we presented the past 3 years' tax returns to a new CPA and he then filed an amendment for the previous 3 years. In that year alone, the tax return for overpaid taxes was more than my annual salary. Get a trusted and trustworthy accountant who works for you and puts the best interest of you and your business first.

DOCUMENT REVIEW WITH AN ATTORNEY

Another area where professionals can help is in document review. Any time you're presented with a contract or agreement, it's important to have an attorney look it over to make sure you're not inadvertently signing away your rights or opening yourself up to liability. By hiring a professional to review documents, you can avoid costly mistakes down the road.

I remember one time recently when I signed a software agreement without having it reviewed by anyone. The company providing the services did not actually perform as they were expected to. However, I didn't read the cancellation clause and we were subject to a $60,000 early termination clause. This made my stomach hurt! Fortunately, I was able to bulldog my way out of that one, but it was close. Never again!

HIRING INSURANCE AGENTS

Another way professionals can save you time and money is by helping you secure the right insurance coverage for your needs. Insurance agents have access to many different carriers and can help you find the one that best meets your needs at the most competitive price.

As I said, this isn't a long chapter, but it is an important one. There are many benefits to hiring professionals to handle different aspects of your business. From saving money on taxes to avoiding costly mistakes, hiring pros can help you run your business more efficiently so that you can focus on what's most important: taking care of patients.

ACTION STEPS:

Are you still trying to do things in your office that a professional should be doing?

Stop it!

Outsource those tasks to save yourself time and money. And if you're not sure whether or not you should outsource a particular task, ask yourself this question: would I do this if it weren't part of my job? If the answer is no, then you probably need to hire a pro.

CHAPTER 19

The More Talented the Doctor, the Crazier the Spouse

First, let me say that I'm only kind of kidding on the title of this chapter. This chapter is devoted to Tricia Sams, who consequently is the wife of Dr. Sams. The two of them have successfully navigated the working relationship for over 23 years. In-fact, if it were not for her, this practice would not be where it is today (for the better). She has faithfully stood by his side for a long time. She read him his textbooks while they commuted and visited family. She traveled with him to many trainings and was his human guinea pig for many experiments/procedures. She is his biggest supporter. All of that to say, they both will admit that one of the reasons that I have a job is because some of the positions she was forced into as the spouse/business partner were not in her skillset. We love her dearly, but just like her very talented husband, she comes with a bit of crazy... which we all love... most of the time. ;-)

You and your spouse have been through a lot together. One or both of you went through some kind of doctoral training and made it through the residencies and rotations. You are finally able to open your own practice. Having your spouse as a business partner in your medical office can have some great benefits, but also some major downfalls. I spoke to a doctor this past week who said, "They sure didn't teach me anything about business in medical school." Maybe the same is true for your spouse.

Oftentimes, working together can lead to marital strife. That is why setting decision boundaries in the relationship is important. Sometimes one spouse is more concerned about certain things while another is more concerned with other things. When you are driving home in the evening, after a long day of work, it can be frustrating that the other is not sharing your same passion in your shared goals. This is why defined boundaries are so important in the business. It's okay for one spouse to not care about where you purchase supplies from and another to not care about the line of supplements you want to carry.

Let's start with the pros of working with your spouse. There are several benefits of working with a spouse, especially in the medical field. One of the biggest benefits is that you know each other very well. Because you know each other so well, you are able to communicate effectively and understand each other's strengths and weaknesses. This can help create a more cohesive work environment because you can play off each other's strengths. Married doctors often make a great team because they are able to provide continuity of care for patients and they have a shared passion for their work.

Another big benefit is that you already have built-in trust with your spouse. In any business relationship, but especially in the medical field, trust is essential. You need to be able to trust that your business partner will make decisions that are in the best interest of the business, even when you are not around. When you are married, there is already a level of trust that exists because you have committed to being honest and loyal to each other in good times and bad times. This can be helpful when making decisions about things like finances and hiring staff.

Now, some of the downfalls of working with your spouse. One of the biggest challenges of working with a spouse is learning how to separate work life from home life. When you are married and working together, it can be difficult to leave work at the office. Oftentimes, arguments or disagreements at work can spill over into your personal life, which can lead to tension and stress in the relationship. It is important to learn how to set boundaries between work life and home life so that you can maintain a healthy balance. Otherwise, it is easy for work to consume every aspect of your life and relationship.

Another big challenge is learning how to disagree without getting personal. Because you know each other so well, it can be easy to let arguments get out of hand quickly because you know exactly which buttons to push with each other. It is important to learn how to disagree without getting personal or emotional so that you can resolve conflicts quickly and efficiently without damaging the relationship.

If you have been in the medical field for any length of time, you have heard the horror stories about the wife who was handling the books of the medical practice and over several years skimmed hundreds of thousands of dollars under the table. She then leaves with a man who is quite similar to the doctor she stole from. I unfortunately have heard this story more than once.

While I would like to say that this is an isolated incident, it unfortunately is not. I have also heard stories of doctors who have met their spouses after they have already started their own medical practices. The new spouse then comes in and takes over the business aspects of things, oftentimes with disastrous results. In some cases, the new spouse has run the practice into the ground financially and the doctor is left with nothing.

While there are certainly some risks involved with marrying someone who is not in the medical field, I believe that the risks are even greater for those who marry another doctor. There are just so many potential conflicts of interest that can arise. For example, what happens if you are both working at the same clinic and one of you gets promoted? Who decides which one of you will stay and which one of you will leave? What happens if one of you wants to start your own practice but the other doesn't? These are just a few of the many questions that can create tension in a relationship when both spouses are doctors.

I believe that it is always best to err on the side of caution when it comes to financial matters, especially when you are in a profession that is known for being sued on a regular basis. I would strongly encourage any doctor who is considering marriage to create a prenuptial agreement. This agreement should outline how the couple's finances will be handled both during the marriage and in the event of a divorce. Without such an agreement, it is all too easy for things to get messy quickly if the relationship ends up going sour.

While no one likes to think about the possibility of their marriage ending in divorce, it is important to be prepared for any eventuality. A prenuptial agreement can give you peace of mind knowing that you will be protected financially if your marriage does not work out. If you are unmarried, I urge you to protect yourself by creating a prenuptial agreement. It could end up being the best decision you ever make. If you are already married and don't have a prenuptial agreement, you both better make sure you are communicating regularly. Your lack of vigilance is no excuse for apathy.

ACTION STEPS:

If you are for sure going to work with your spouse, here are some things you may want to consider:

1. First, take inventory of your strengths and weaknesses. What does each of you bring to the table? Make a list and be honest with yourselves.

2. You will need to decide who is going to do what in the business. It is important to have clearly defined roles. Trying to do it all will lead to burnout for both of you.

3. In the early years, you will likely be working long hours. This can put a strain on your relationship. You may need to schedule some time for just the two of you.

4. Money can be a big issue when you are in business together. You will need to set some decision boundaries in your relationship. Who has final say on spending? What are the limits?

5. Finally, remember that you are in this together. You will need to be each other's biggest supporters.

If you can successfully navigate these issues, you will be able to have a successful business and a happy marriage.

CHAPTER 20

It's a Real Business, Treat it Like One

THE IMPORTANCE OF PROFESSIONALISM IN A SMALL BUSINESS

As a small business grows, it is important to maintain a level of professionalism. Often times, businesses get stuck in the "mom and pop" mentality, which can prevent growth. In this chapter, we will talk about the importance of making decisions for a small business that will scale as you grow.

For the sake of conversation, let's first define the difference between growth and scale. Growth is the increase in the number of employees, customers, sales, etc. Scale is the ability to maintain that growth over time. A business can grow without scaling, but it will eventually hit a ceiling. To scale a business means to be able to handle that growth long term.

I had to change my mindset a few years ago that I no longer wanted to grow, I actually wanted to scale! As we were growing, I noticed the block tower getting more wobbly because we actually couldn't sustain that growth.

Most of us have been there as a small company. We made some easy decisions that just make sense. A silly example we talk about at the office lately is what to do on a "snow day." As the owners of the clinic are from Iowa, there is not really such a thing as a "snow day." If it snowed, Dr. Sams would get out his 4-wheel drive and pick up the office gal and they would treat anyone who ventured out that day. During the quiet times, they would do a deep cleaning of closets and drawers. At lunch, the company would buy the three of them lunch and they would close up early and happy. Fast forward to today. If it snows and people just show up to work, that hourly clock is clipping on in the many hundreds of dollars an hour. It becomes expensive to just sit there and wait on the next patient to show up. It is actually more advantageous to close the office on a snow day in our current situation than to have the payroll clock spinning at wind-making speeds.

Here is my top 10 small business decisions that will help you scale in the future.

1. Hire a professional accountant or bookkeeper early on. This will ensure that your financial records are accurate and up-to-date, which will be helpful if you ever need to secure financing or make big financial decisions. It also will help you with your taxes. Prior to my working at the office, they paid their accountant a small fortune because the office's books were in shambles.

2. Get liability insurance. I know this sounds like a no-brainer, but this will protect your business from lawsuits and other claims that may arise from your products or services. Also, make sure your malpractice insurance covers any of the new services you have added since taking out the policy.

3. Create standard operating procedures (SOPs). SOPs are step-by-step guides that outline how to do specific tasks within your business. Having SOPs in place will help new employees learn their roles quickly and efficiently, and it will also help keep your business running smoothly if

you ever need to take a vacation or take some time off. When I have a quality staff member, I often ask them to write their own SOP. I make them divide it in sections of Daily Tasks, Weekly Tasks, Monthly Tasks, Yearly Tasks, and PRN Tasks.

4. Invest in marketing and advertising. A professional website and well-executed marketing campaign can go a long way in helping you attract new customers and grow your business. The rule of thumb in the medical industry is that you may need to spend up to 11% of every dollar made on marketing.

5. Build strong relationships with suppliers and vendors. Establishing good relationships with the companies you do business with can lead to better terms, discounts, and other perks that can save your business money.

6. Develop a customer retention strategy. It costs more to attract new customers than it does to keep existing ones, so it's important to have a plan in place for retaining your best customers. Offering loyalty programs, discounts, and other incentives can help keep your customers coming back for more. We talk about this throughout the book.

7. Implement a human resources management system. As your business grows, you'll need to start tracking employee information such as contact information, performance reviews, time off requests, etc. Having an HR system in place will make it easier to manage this information and stay compliant with labor laws.

8. Foster a culture of innovation within your organization . Encourage employees to come up with new ideas and ways to improve customer experience or increase efficiency. Try implementing an employee suggestions program where every month you ask employees fill out forms with their suggestions then review them to pick the best ones to implement.

9. Promote work / life balance for employees. Create policies that encourage employees to take vacation days, leave early on Fridays, etc. Many people who want a work life balance will seek out employers who offer it.

10. Focus on employee development and training. Properly trained employees benefit both the employer (through increased productivity & quality of work) and themselves (by gaining skills making them more marketable & more earning potential). Look into webinar trainings, podcasts, etc. for relevant industry trends and changes taking place that can help employees feel valued and keep them engaged and motivated. We have started doing a lunch-n-learn every three weeks at the office. Some are BYOL (Bring Your Own Lunch) while others are provided by a vendor, etc.

By making decisions that will scale as you grow, and implementing the right systems and processes early on, you can set your small business up for success! Professionalism is key in order to build a successful small business that will stand the test of time!

ACTION STEPS:

What are some antiquated ideas that you have that are holding your business back?

How can you start to build systems and processes that will scale as your business grows?

What are some ways you can foster a culture of innovation within your organization?

What are some ways you can promote work / life balance for employees?

What are some ways you can focus on employee development and training?

CHAPTER 21

How and When to Fire a Patient

I picked up another nugget of wisdom from that class I told you about previously called "How to Fire a Volunteer." I'm telling you, this concept was liberating in my life. Obviously, the class was about how to get rid of a person whom you weren't paying that was helping you out in your work. For me, I was able to take these same concepts and apply them to patient relationships.

There is a false belief in the business world that "the customer is always right." I don't believe this to be true. I always want to respect my patients, but I militantly protect my staff and providers. I don't allow patients to disrespect them nor manipulate them. Truth be told, when I protect my staff and providers, and specifically publicly defend them, that goes a long way! It is easier for me to find a new patient than it is to recruit and train new staff, and especially providers!

There might come a time when you need to "fire a patient." The funny thing is, our culture thinks that this isn't something that can even be done. Trust me, it can be done and it should be done.

Here are some guidelines for how to know when it is time to "fire" a patient from your practice:

1. The patient is constantly complaining and is never happy with anything.

2. The patient is disrespectful to you, your staff, or your providers.

3. The patient is always trying to get something for free or get out of paying their bill.

4. The patient is constantly calling or coming in for things that are not medically necessary.

5. The patient refuses to follow your treatment plan or advice.

These are just a few examples, but I'm sure you can think of more. The bottom line is that if a patient is causing more harm than good, it might be time to let them go.

Don't be afraid to "fire" a patient if it is in the best interest of your practice. It might seem daunting, but it is really quite simple. Just explain to the patient that you feel like it would be better for them to get care elsewhere and politely ask them to leave. It is that simple.

You shouldn't feel guilty about "firing" a patient. You are doing them a favor by getting them the care they need from someone who can better meet their needs. And you are doing a favor for your practice by getting rid of a toxic person.

Just because you did it with a smile, don't think that there might not be repercussions to your practice including a violent departure from the building, a social media retaliation, or the necessity to call the police to have the person removed from your property (Yes, all of these have had to happen). Keep in mind that you will need to be able to provide continuity of care through your notes to whomever is going to care for them.

Though there isn't some kind of legal document signed at the beginning of care, we document via a letter to them that we are dismissing them from our care. We also make sure this is noted in their chart and that letter is added to their record at our office. I also make sure to tell my staff (especially those making appointments) that a patient is no longer to be seen at our office.

This way, they can be redirected if they should call or come in.

ACTION STEPS:

FIRING A PATIENT

1. If you haven't already, take some time to develop a policy for dismissing patients from your practice.

2. When you have determined that it is time to dismiss a patient, sit down with them and explain why you feel it would be better for them to get care elsewhere.

3. Be prepared for anything! The person could react angrily or violently. It is always best to have someone else in the room with you when doing this.

4. Send the patient a certified letter confirming that they are no longer welcome at your practice and that their records will be made available to them upon request.

5. Make sure to document everything in the patient's chart and keep a copy of the dismissal letter in their file.

6. Tell your staff (in person or via email) that the patient is no longer welcome at your practice and provide them with a brief explanation as to why.

7. Finally, don't beat yourself up over it! You did what was best for your practice and for the patient.

Who are the patients you need to fire?

CHAPTER 22

Policies Matter: The Importance of Developing a Policy and Procedure Manual in a Medical Office

Many times when doctors are faced with a lawsuit, they are shocked to learn that their conduct was the subject of a formal complaint or that their behavior could have been seen as negligent. They ask themselves, "What could I have done to prevent this?" In most cases, the answer is simple: develop and maintain policies and procedures.

Policies and procedures protect both the doctor and the medical practice. They help to ensure that patients are treated fairly and consistently, that doctors maintain high standards of care, and that the medical practice avoids potential legal liability. While some policies and procedures are required by law or regulation, others are best practices that should be adopted by all medical practices.

WHAT IS A POLICY?

A policy is a formal statement of principles that guide the decisions and actions of those who work in a medical practice. Policies can be general in nature or specific to a particular area such as patient confidentiality or prescribing controlled substances. For example, a policy on patient confidentiality would state that all employees must keep patient information confidential except when required by law or with the patient's consent. A policy on prescribing controlled substances would set out the conditions under which controlled substances may be prescribed and specify who is authorized to prescribe them.

WHAT IS A PROCEDURE?

A procedure is a set of detailed instructions for carrying out a task or series of tasks. Procedures can be general in nature or specific to a particular area such as infection control or billing. For example, a procedure for infection control would describe how to properly wash your hands and what to do if you come into contact with blood or other bodily fluids. A procedure for billing would describe how to generate invoices and how to handle payments from patients.

WHY ARE POLICIES AND PROCEDURES IMPORTANT?

Policies and procedures are important because they help to ensure that patients are treated fairly and consistently, that doctors maintain high standards of care, and that the medical practice avoids potential legal liability.

For example, let's say that a doctor makes a mistake while performing surgery and the patient sues the doctor for negligence. One of the first things the lawyer for the patient will look at is the policies and procedures of the medical practice to see if there were any deviations from standard care. If there was no deviation, then it will be more difficult for the lawyer to prove that the doctor was negligent. However, if the lawyer can find evidence that the doctor deviated from accepted policies and procedures, then it will be easier to prove negligence.

Another reason why policies and procedures are important is because they help to ensure compliance with laws and regulations. For example, federal law requires all healthcare providers who bill Medicare/Medicaid to have written policies and procedures in place regarding billing practices. These policies and procedures must be followed in order for healthcare providers to avoid False Claims Act liability.

Your practice's policy and procedure guidelines can be as simple or as complex as you want, but it's important to have them in writing so that you and your team agree with the vision you've set for your practice.

Having a standard, well-organized policy structure helps employees navigate policies more easily. With the rapid pace of new and updated laws and regulations that vendors are facing, the task of keeping policies and procedures up to date, accessible, and effectively disseminated throughout the organization can be very challenging. With the ever-increasing number of new rules and regulations such as the Affordable Care Act, HIPAA, and rational use, the burden of defining policies and effectively communicating them to employees has become heavy. While regulations, third-party payer requirements, and licensing/accreditation standards exacerbate this complexity, formalized policies and procedures can mitigate it, promoting health and safety, regulatory compliance, and providing high-quality, safe, and reliable patient care.

The importance of medical office policies and procedures cannot be disputed, but the way they are best managed varies from organization to organization. The main goal of these policies and procedures is to establish a high degree of mutual understanding, cooperation, efficiency, and unity among staff and providers. It is important that all people in the healthcare organization participate in the development and implementation of policies and procedures and understand what they are and how they are used.

A detailed policy and procedure guide is a valuable communication tool for efficiently processing all business transactions within an organization and reducing data transmission gaps. A documented procedure guide not only saves time in identifying processes, it also reduces errors and increases employee productivity.

Your procedures should include enough detail so that a new employee can complete the task based on the information provided. In your manual, you should find policies for the entire company, for individual parts of the company, and for individual employees. The rules in your manual are essential to the success of your practice and the care of your patients. Be wary of adopting a topic-specific policy or practice that simply states that staff must adhere to the practices outlined in the ABC Handbook (and does not describe the organization's steps).

Each policy must include a disclaimer to remind employees that they must use their own judgment to determine if all parts of the policy and procedure apply to each situation or if any change is required.

By having someone in your medical practice update and review your new office manual at least once a year, you will help keep your practice up to date and track how you achieve your goals and milestones, which will improve your practice for years to come. The medical office employee handbook contains the rules of medical practice for employees. All well-written and comprehensive practice policy manual includes procedures for communication with patients and relationships.

Finally, policies and procedures help communicate expectations to employees regarding their conduct at work. For example, if an employee violates a policy or procedure, then he or she can be disciplined up to and including termination depending on the severity of the violation. However, if an employee is not aware of a policy or procedure, then he or she cannot as easily be held accountable for violating it.

ACTION STEPS:

Do you have a Policy Manual?

Do you have a Procedures Manual?

When were the last time they were updated?

Who is responsible for updating them?

What needs to be in your Policy Manual?

What needs to be in your Procedures Manual?

How will you get employees to read and follow the manuals?

Enforcement - What are the consequences for not following the policies and procedures?

Need help with this? See our contact information in the last chapter.

CHAPTER 23

Your Office Stinks

Have you ever heard of the term "nose blind?" Nose blind actually means that your nose gets used to smells around you and tunes them out. But what if the smell is so strong that even your nose can't ignore it? If you work in an office, chances are you've come across some pretty rank smells. Maybe it's the guy in the office next to you who never showers, or the co-worker who's always wearing too much cologne. Whatever the source, office smells can be pretty gross.

I remember as a kid, you could totally tell which kid passed gas because it had the undertone of the fabric softener that his mom used. I used to call him out on passing gas and he was amazed that I could tell that it was him... every time! I think my oldest daughter is a bloodhound. Sometimes she will come up to you sniffing and figure out the food that you have eaten recently or the restaurant you were in. Certain people have heightened olfactory senses, but many patients have real medical conditions that can attribute to a sensitivity to smells. Many of your MTHFR patients are hyper-sensitive to smells and especially the smells in your office or on your person.

If you're stuck dealing with a smelly office, there are a few things you can do to try to improve the situation. Let's look at this in three different categories: Environmental, Structural, and Chemical.

ENVIRONMENTAL

Environmental smells can come from outside or inside your building. If you have a smoking section near your office, that could be the source of the smell. If there are unfinished food items in the garbage, that could also account for smells. If it's coming from outside, talk to your landlord about the issue. They may not be aware that there is a problem. If it's coming from inside the building, see if there is anything you can do to clean up the area. Sometimes just a little bit of elbow grease can make a big difference.

STRUCTURAL

There are some smells that come from the structure of the building itself. This could be things like old carpets or musty air. If the source of the smell is structural, it may be more difficult to get rid of. You may need to talk to your landlord or building manager about making some changes. In some cases, you may be able to make a small change that can make a big difference. For example, if the carpet is the problem, you may be able to put down some area rugs. This can help to absorb some of the smell and make the space more bearable. A dehumidifier in a crawl-space or a professional to do hydrogen peroxide treatment can work wonders.

CHEMICAL

Many fragrances and perfumes are made from chemicals that can be toxic. These chemicals can off-gas and cause problems for people with sensitivities. If you're concerned about the chemicals in your office, you can try to find natural alternatives. There are now many essential oils and other natural products that can be used to make a space smell nice. You can also try to avoid using fragrances yourself. Many people are sensitive to perfumes and colognes, so it's best to err on the side of caution.

At our office, we have a no-fragrances policy for our staff and patients. This helps to create a safe and welcoming environment for everyone. This includes body sprays, colognes, perfumes, etc.

While some smells are just unpleasant, others can actually be dangerous. Many fragrances and perfumes contain chemicals that have been linked to health problems. These chemicals can off-gas and cause respiratory problems, headaches, and even cancer.

I remember being adjusted by a chiropractor who obviously had a BUNCH of cologne on his hands and it got all over my face. My eyes were stinging. I had to go home and shower before I went anywhere else because this man didn't have the decency to not pollute the air. This is a job, not a date.

We have a patient who almost had to be taken to the hospital because of another patient's cologne. This same patient came in the other day about 30 minutes after a staff member made microwave popcorn. Her pulse ox dropped and she wasn't breathing well. For these, and many other reasons, we have a no fragrances policy in the office.

Look at all the items in your office that have a "scent." These include lotions, emollients, soaps, air fresheners, fabric softeners, hand sanitizers, laundry detergent, and even your trash sacks. I encourage you to consider switching to unscented or natural options for these products. This can help to create a more pleasant environment for everyone.

Before you ask, yes, I have asked a patient who was wearing an off-putting cologne to shower and come back another time.

PERFUMES, COLOGNES, LOTIONS, & TOBACCO

Perfumes and colognes today are not made from flower or plant extracts. They're made from more than 4,000 different toxic chemicals, 95% of which come from petroleum. Many of our patients and staff are highly sensitive to perfumes and chemicals, including residual toxins from tobacco products. For this reason, we ask that you please refrain from wearing perfume, cologne, aftershave, or scented lotions when visiting our office, and that you please refrain from smoking the day of your appointment. You may be asked to reschedule your appointment if you fail to do so.

Section from Patient Handbook regarding scents

Here is the exact wording of my staff policy manual regarding this topic:

> Employees must report for work clean and well groomed. Offensive body odor, bad breath or use of perfumes, bodysprays and colognes are inappropriate for our desired image and close working situations. If necessary this will be addressed privately with the employee and the employees asked to immediately remedy their odor.

ACTION STEPS:

Do you have any environmental smelly items you need to clean up?

What are they?

Do you have any structural smelly items you need to clean up?

What are they?

What items are you using in your practice that have an artificial fragrance?

How can you eliminate or reduce the amount of these items?

What is your policy on fragrances in your office?

Make sure your staff and patients are aware of this policy.

Enforce this policy.

A game-changer that we have found that really helps remediate smells and purifies the air is an o-zone generator, which you can purchase on Amazon. There are good ones and bad ones. Some make the air smell burned. I really like the ones from EcoQuest. https://ecoquestpurifiers.com/.

CHAPTER 24

Cut Your Expenses

I'm actually known for saving money. Sometimes this is to a fault. In fact, some of the chapters of this book have been created because of good (and bad) lessons I have learned from my "frugalness." Sometimes it was totally worth it. Other times, the time spent and the money saved do not equate.

Unfortunately, in a growing medical practice, you have to keep an eye on those expenses. Even when you think you have things under control, you need to be looking at things periodically in order to make sure you are getting the best deals.

This is a minor example, but the amount of money that our office used to spend on appointment reminder cards was 3 times more than what we are currently spending. I saw a bill come across my desk for $300 for business cards (appointment reminder cards). I thought to myself, did we order 10,000? We had not. Actually, the person in charge of ordering, just went to a place that was overcharging and not providing great quality. We changed vendors and now get these cards for $100.

There are many areas of your practice that you might be overspending on. Reducing operating costs can save your practice thousands of dollars a year. Your office is a business, and trying to cut down on the operating costs can sometimes be a daunting task. With ever-increasing changes in government and private pay reimbursement, it's surprising how many doctors' offices haven't taken the time to explore ways to reduce overhead and operating costs. In order for practitioners to reduce operating costs and become more profitable, they must take the counterintuitive step of updating existing technology too, especially when organizing and managing patient records is a priority.

Many small practices and lone practitioners have already made significant efforts in the past to increase profitability by reducing incremental costs and other operating costs. The end result is cost savings that all medical practices can benefit from. Every business, big or small, new or mature, can benefit from daily cost reductions. For doctors' offices, cutting some of these day-to-day expenses means more money can be devoted to patient care and support, or even your pocketbook.

One of the most effective ways to reduce overhead costs is to optimize registration and billing for the services provided. When a hospital operation reduces avoidable overhead while investing in high-value overheads it will increase the competitiveness of their facilities. The same is true with your small-office. All business owners want to cut costs, but as a healthcare professional, you want to make sure your services don't suffer.

Your financial resources can be depleted due to utility costs, office maintenance, and office space rent. Renting office space, paying utility bills, and maintaining a physical office can result in an outflow of financial resources. We moved to a new office that was 3 times the size of the property we were previously in. The new facility has 90 solar panels on its roof. I was amazed that our electric bill at this new place is about 66% less than it was in the place that was 3 times smaller.

Another way to cut costs is to check the location of the office and compare it with available real estate. You can renegotiate lease or lease terms based on changing market conditions and land prices in your business area to save on operating costs. Operating expenses allow you to examine in detail how your costs affect your bottom line.

You must identify the root causes of high costs and implement smart and creative solutions to improve your finances and thrive through value-based care. You need to recognize the cost problem, identify the sources of the problem, and then start on the road to improvement. While cost issues seem out of control and are getting worse, doctor's offices can minimize them with new creative approaches to how they operate clinics and handle finances.

To address these minor issues, medical practices must change their business models to focus on costs. For years, our office was able to make easier decisions because we were a small practice. As we have gotten bigger, our decisions have become more costly. I think back to things we used to do that we are no longer doing. We are outsourcing certain things like HR, landscaping, payroll, accounting, and more.

There are several areas in which research can reduce smaller costs, which together add up to big savings. You may be surprised, but being vigilant about inefficiencies can go a long way in reducing operating costs. Whether it's eliminating some of the costs of labor, depreciation, supplies, insurance, etc., you need to be as efficient as possible to make a profit. Instead, by strategically thinking about where processes can run more efficiently, how best to use people's skills, and where it makes sense to eliminate redundant resources, practitioners can save money and deliver a higher quality of service.

Create a website that patients can use to pay their bills, book appointments, request refills of prescriptions/supplements online, and download forms and educational materials (saving paperwork on printing costs). Educate your staff on how patient portals can save on research costs, and then educate patients about their use and benefits. This eliminates the need for patients to send payments by mail and helps reduce costs by reducing billing costs.

ACTION STEPS:

You may need to sit down and really look at your expenses and costs. Once you understand your costs, you can look at several methods to start cutting costs and increasing profits. Intuit (the makers of QuickBooks) has a list of ideas to help you reduce operating expenses and generate more revenue *(my thoughts in italics)*:

- Automate time-consuming tasks.
    - *What are things you are doing over and over again that could be automated?*
        - *Employee onboarding?*
        - *Making a handout that describes the same speech you gave 100 times a week?*
        - *Inventory Management?*
        - *Auto-remind phone calls/texts?*
        - *Automated email processes?*
- Outsource for extra efficiency.
    - *Do the math and see if you can outsource some of your work.*
        - *I.T.*
        - *Advertising*
        - *Mailing Services*
        - *Newsletters*
        - *Copywriting*
        - *Billing*
        - *Appointment Setting*
- Find a freelancer.
    - *Even though you CAN do something, it doesn't mean that you should!*
    - *What is your time worth?*
    - *Have you looked into www.fiverr.com or other freelance websites?*
- Integrate an internship.
    - *In our therapy department, we started getting students who came for their clinical rotations. Not only were we able to*

invest in the upcoming generation, we were able to get 8 weeks (per student) of free labor!

- Entertain different vendor bids.
  - *Make sure you are pricing things out on occasion. Don't be afraid to put bids against each other and see who wants the business more!*
- Ditch your office building.
  - *Sometimes your building and location is an asset, and other times it is a liability. Only you can know this, but don't be afraid to ask the question.*
- Pay your bills in advance.
  - *Are you paying interest on things you don't need to be paying interest on?*
  - *Do you have leases that you could easily pay off and you choose to pay the extra money so you didn't have to let go of any of your own?*
    - *Analyze this.*
- Put wasteful habits to rest.
  - *Are there old spending habits that need to go away?*
- Pull the plug on unused services.
  - *Do you have recurring memberships and auto-pays that you don't use anymore, but you are too busy to cancel?*
- Use free apps whenever possible.
  - *We automated our timeclock software with an old iPhone and free software.*
- Go paperless.
  - *For a paperless office, we sure do print a lot! I'm not sure about this, but paper is a mess and can cost you a lot in labor for time spent filing, etc.*
- Use bartering instead of cash.
  - *For some services, bartering may be the way to go. Here is a silly example out of our office. Our primary doctor is too busy to break away for a haircut. His barber doesn't take appointments so by leaving during the day, he might miss up to four*

patient visits. Instead, we book the barber on an end-of-day appointment and he brings his stuff, cuts the doctor's hair, and we barter out an adjustment. It's a win-win for us.

Though we both could argue some of these for your specific office, they are some pretty good standards to live by.

One last area to look at is an entity called a GPO or Group Purchasing Organization. Look them up and see which ones you might qualify for. I joined a GPO (for no cost) and immediately saved 1% annually on our credit card transactions which equated to about $9,000 annually.

CHAPTER 25

'Them's My Niches – Looking at High-ticket Items

It can be difficult to bring in new patients, and even more difficult to keep existing patients. In order to expand your practice, you may want to consider bringing in specialty niches. Specialty niches are a great way to attract new patients, as well as retain existing patients. Not only that, but they can also be incredibly profitable.

HOW MUCH MONEY CAN YOU MAKE WITH SPECIALTY NICHES?

The amount of money you can make with specialty niches will depend on a number of factors, such as the niche you choose and the size of your practice. Also, it will greatly depend on how good at sales you are, or more so, if you are willing to hire someone who is better at sales than you are. However, if done correctly, specialty niches can be extremely profitable. For example, take neuropathy. Many practices across the nation charge around $6,000 for a neuropathy package with a cost of about $3,000 per package. If you were able to sell one neuropathy package per week for 52 weeks, that's an additional $156,000 in PROFIT per year. And that's just for one niche being sold to ONLY 52 people in a year! You could easily have multiple specialty niches bringing in that much money or more. You can also piggyback the niches to generate more income.

WHAT ARE SOME GOOD SPECIALTY NICHES TO CONSIDER?

There are a number of good specialty niches to consider for your medical practice. Below is a list of some popular ones:

- Neuropathy
- Erectile Dysfunction
- PRP and Stem Cells
- Weight Loss
- Liposuction Alternatives
- Functional Medicine
- Gut Health
- Decompression
- Sports Medicine
- Pediatrics
- Hormone Pellet Therapy
- Geriatrics
- Women's Health
- Mental Health
- Rehabilitation Medicine
- Occupational Medicine
- Pain Management

These are just a few ideas to get you started. When choosing a specialty niche for your practice, it is important to choose one that you are passionate about and that will be profitable. For example, weight loss is a popular choice for many doctors because it is both profitable and rewarding. However, if you're not passionate or compassionate about working with overweight people, then it may not be the best choice for you. The same goes for any other specialty niche. Choose one that interests you and that you feel comfortable with. Only then will you be able to provide quality care to your patients and maximize your profits.

I mentioned this earlier in the book, but we added hormone pellet therapy through a company called bioTE. The average pelleted person brings 7 new patients into your office to receive pellets, and done correctly, you can have a greater than 90% retention rate of your patients throughout their lifetime. That is a good long-term gain!

Specializing in a particular area can help set your practice apart from the competition and attract new patients. Not only that, but it can also be incredibly profitable. If you're thinking about specializing in a particular area, we encourage you to do some research and choose one that interests you and that has the potential to be profitable.

Many would say that niches are the way to go to grow your practice and lessen the physical load of working. Less patients for more money.

ACTION STEPS:

Are you currently offering any niches?

Do you have the appropriate "sales" team in place?

Is your staff trained to help you with these services?

Are you successfully converting these patients into niche services?

What niches would you like to start offering?

CHAPTER 26

Trust the Science / It's Still Science

Depending on the type of practice you are operating, and especially if it is more natural or Eastern Medicine leaning, people are quick to question the validity of what you do. I often have to remind people that just because you don't like the "science" that we are operating under, it doesn't mean that it isn't science! The most famous example of this story is Nikola Tesla and Thomas Edison and their voltage war.

The two greatest inventors of all time are Nikola Tesla and Thomas Edison. The transmission systems of each company competed for dominance. There has been a war between alternating current and direct current. Electricity was the subject of a clash between two visions in the nineteenth century: Nikola Tesla, who favored alternating current (AC), and Thomas Alba Edison, who favored direct current (DC). The newspaper headlines at the time referred to this battle as The War of the Currents.

In electricity, electrons continually move from a positive to a negative pole. As alternating current and direct current flow differently, these electrons behave differently:

- The flow of direct current is stable and unidirectional, so it does not vary over time. Batteries store current in them.
- The alternating current circulates cyclically, fluctuating in magnitude and direction periodically. We use this current to power our homes through the power lines.

ADVANTAGES OF DIRECT CURRENT

It is safer to use direct current than alternating current due to its tendency to be consistent. The insulation requirements are lower, and it is possible to use lower voltages. Batteries can also be used to store them.

ADVANTAGES OF ALTERNATING CURRENT

Over long distances, alternating current is more energy-efficient than direct current because it loses less energy. Direct current can also be easily converted from it. Direct current is safer than the alternating current in terms of transmission and transformation.

There were qualitative and quantitative advances in electricity during the 19th century. The energy demand was increasing, power plants were being built bigger and longer, and there was an increasing need for long-distance energy transmission. It was necessary to power ever-larger cities and industries in the vast American West.

As a result of the dissipation of part of the energy as heat, Edison advocated direct current, which was more expensive and inefficient. Alternating current was, on the other hand, preferred by Nikola Tesla. This was the beginning of their rivalry.

According to Tesla, Edison's direct current was inefficient and more expensive. Energy is lost along the way as the distance increases. To improve this system, Tesla proposed his own: alternating current.

Tesla's idea meant electricity could be transmitted over long distances at a high voltage without energy loss. When it reached its destination, medium- and low-voltage distribution could be done quickly and inexpensively using transformers. In today's world, power stations deliver electricity to homes through this system.

From a financial perspective, JP Morgan and George Westinghouse Jr. were at war. Formerly, for the country's electrification with direct current, he was partnered with Thomas Edison, while later, with Tesla.

Even though Edison's system was less efficient, he would have lost much money by switching. In the wake of Tesla's obvious advantages, the company won increasing contracts. Nevertheless, he faced a serious obstacle: the high voltages of alternating current caused several fatal accidents among engineers and operators. Tesla and his alternating current were discredited by Edison's supporters through several widely read newspapers, with each death as an excuse.

One of Edison's dirty dealings included public demonstrations in the style of a circus, where his supporters stunned an animal, first with mild currents. As soon as the current was applied, the victim was electrocuted by a high voltage alternating current. People were being made afraid of the consequences of electrifying a country with the alternating current for no good reason. The propaganda war was lost by Tesla.

Alternating current, though, became the best system for electrifying the country, and additional safety measures were added to substations and power lines. Niagara Falls' electrical installations were based on it as well as the Chicago World's Fair in 1893.

Since Tesla was obliged to sell his patent to Westinghouse, he could not enjoy the fruits of victory. However, Edison's company, already renamed General Electric, implicitly conceded defeat in its effort to electrify the nation by acquiring Westinghouse patents.

Tesla was consigned to oblivion even though he "won" the war. The Tesla coil and wireless lighting are examples of his "extravagant" inventions, to which he continued to devote his time. He failed to translate his ideas into practical advances because they were ahead of their time. A reclusive and eccentric scientist, he died penniless. On the other hand, Edison became a millionaire thanks to several patents, such as those on the light bulb and the phonograph. The inventor has become one of history's most admired and well-known figures.

They both had science and they both had a purpose. Own the fact that whatever element of practice you are operating is backed by science. Learn the science, trust the science, and don't be ashamed of the science. Don't get into a fight as to why "your" science is better. Realize that other sciences may have a place at the table, just maybe not your table. And that is okay!

If Eastern Medicine or natural-leaning practitioners would maturely and responsibly stand behind their science and Western Medicine practitioners would realize that things like TCM (Traditional Chinese Medicine) have been around millennia longer than their craft, we might just be able to all get along in the same sandbox...

I'm not saying we have to build the same sandcastles, just quit throwing sand at each other's eyes!

ACTION STEPS:

Learn your science.

Quit throwing sand!

CHAPTER 27

Setting Goals and Sticking to Them

When I was younger, I used to hate it when people would have me write down my goals. I'm not sure why, but I didn't like it. That page would always be blank on my conference notebook. It really irritated my wife. My wife knows I don't like to do this, and I know she loves to do it. One night when we were newlyweds, she wanted to go to bed early and was really tired. Right as she was drifting off to sleep, I said, "Let's talk about our marriage goals." Unfortunately for me, that woke her right up and she laid out some goals. I wasn't ready for that!

The same is true about your business. You must set goals. You must revisit those goals. Without a target, you are just firing at the air. From 2017 to 2021 we doubled the gross revenue of our practice. I threw down the gauntlet to my staff in January of 2022 that I wanted to double the practice again by the end of 2023. They know this goal. I talk about this goal. I remind them when they aren't helping me reach this goal.

I recently sat down with Dan Tieman with StealthMedia who I hired to help me reach a goal in my physical therapy department. He asked, "What is your goal with physical therapy?" I told him that I wanted that department to bill over $1,000,000 in a single year. He started asking me some questions and we determined that my monetary goal would not actually be able to be achieved without additional staffing. I loved the direction this gave me. He told me to stop doing some of the things I was doing and to work on staffing first. This allowed me to better utilize my time and reach my goal.

Let's talk about the importance and the reasons why we need to set growth goals in our practice.

1. A goal gives you a target to shoot for.

2. A goal holds you accountable.

3. A goal gives you a sense of accomplishment when you reach it.

4. A goal gives you something to strive for.

5. Goals help keep your business focused.

6. Goals can be used as a marketing and advertising tool. Example: We need 20 new patients this month to reach our goal.

I like to set goals with my providers annually, what I have heard called "HAGS."

1HAG (1 Month Hairy Audacious Goal)

3HAG (3 Month...)

6HAG (6 Month...)

12HAG (12 Month...)

18HAG (18 Month...)

BHAG (BIG HAIRY AUDACIOUS GOAL)

We talk about them as a staff. A "#HAG" can't be something easily attainable, but you still need to be able to reach it. The BHAG is "sky's the limit." Every January at our provider's meeting I have them lay out their HAGs. I also make them do this personally as well. Then throughout the year I cheer for them as they reach these goals. I try to bring them up in conversation. That reminds me, it's about time to bring them up again!

There is a funny (and astrologically incorrect) saying that goes like this:

Shoot for the moon, even if you miss you will be among the stars.

This can be applied to your practice goals.

Yes, you need to have goals that challenge you and your staff, but if you don't reach them, at least you will be in a much better spot than where you started.

When I was in high school, we were required to learn how to juggle in order to pass health class, which was a required class to graduate. We literally had to learn to juggle in order to graduate high school. I asked the teacher one time why we were doing this. He explained it was to teach us the concept of success through our failures. I remember spending hours at home with three rolled up socks trying to juggle. For what seemed like months, I would go in and try to test out of the juggling. For months, I failed. Eventually, I got all of the required 10 catches and passed the class. I was in the clinic recently at a pediatric therapy screening and I was able to juggle for the kids. They were impressed. This was definitely a success through my failures!

I don't know about you, but when I know I am accountable to someone, I tend to do a better job. I remember this guy I knew years ago who held me accountable to certain life choices when I was college aged. He would ask me all these questions and then at the end, he would say, "What did you just lie to me about?" When you know that you have to answer that question at the end, it makes you really think about the answers you are giving.

You need to have people in your life that you are accountable to, even if it is just a friend that will ask you about your goals. But if you really want to be successful, you need to have someone that will not only ask you about your goals, but will also help you develop a plan to reach those goals. This could be a business coach, a consultant, or even another doctor that you look up to.

I challenge you to set some HAGs for your practice this year. And if you need help holding yourself accountable, give me a call. I would love to help you grow your practice!

ACTION STEPS:

What are your goals?

What does your staff know about your goals?

If they don't know, how will they help you achieve those goals?

Take some time this week and sit down with your staff and discuss your goals and their goals for the year. Write them down and put them in a place where everyone can see them.

Who is going to help you achieve your goals?

Do you have someone that will hold you accountable?

If not, find someone or hire someone. It will be worth it!

Our contact information is in the last chapter.

CHAPTER 28

The Importance of a Google Review

I have a love/hate relationship with Google reviews, or any reviews for that matter. I totally know and believe in their importance, but they are a pain to nurture, and sometimes an even bigger pain to control.

I had a meeting recently with a theme park executive. I asked him how things were going at the park and he mentioned how hard it is to run a theme park based upon Google and Trip Advisor reviews. He said that too often large companies are having to play defense (we talked about this earlier in the book) when it comes to reviews. If you ever want to get a real laugh, Google the term "1 star national park reviews." One of my favorites is the 1-star review of Yellowstone because of the lack of mobile phone service.

Google reviews play an important role in your visibility on Google Search, in your overall healthcare Internet marketing strategy, and in acquiring new patients. In other words, your Google reviews help patients see value in your business, what you offer, and a non-filtered look at what it is like to come into your healthcare practice to get treatment. As a result, Google reviews may often be a crucial element when patients are choosing between two different medical practices.

When choosing between two medical practices, one that has hundreds of favorable Google reviews and the other that has only a few reviews, it is easy to understand which one the patient will pick.

I recently chose to see a specific Endocrinologist in Springfield, Missouri because the other ones in town were very poorly rated.

If you have lots of good reviews on Google, you are going to see patients feeling more confident in their choices and decision to come see you for their health needs. This means that the more patient reviews you have, the higher up on Google you will be in terms of rankings for your most relevant keywords related to your medical practice. As it turns out, Google reviews are quite powerful when it comes to growing your patient practice. Online reviews are the digital equivalent of word-of-mouth, and your reputation can go a long way in driving patients into (or out of) your practice.

Patient reviews have gone a long way from merely recommending through word-of-mouth, to publishing an online rating that sifts through your practices. Review/reputation management can also help your healthcare practice bounce back after devastating negative reviews, and maybe even more important, can help you accumulate hundreds of positive reviews on the internet. While it might be impossible to ignore certain negative reviews, it is important for your medical practice to have a way of identifying satisfied patients and encouraging positive reviews in order to counteract any bad ones. Responding to reviews of your practice, whether they are negative or positive, is a great way to establish goodwill and trust, as well as to show patients you care about what is being said.

If you feel any of your patients appear happy with your services, ask them to leave a positive review on Google online. These positive Google reviews will not only help to boost your online reputation, but most importantly, they will bring more patients into your practice. If you encourage more patients to write reviews on Google and other platforms, this helps the search engines gauge how well your reputation is doing against competitors in order to rank you better. Doctors can encourage patients to leave reviews on sites such as Google or Facebook and boost their online reputation, build credibility, and grow their practice.

These reviews help patients learn more about your practice and they boost your search engine rankings. Adding patient reviews on the websites of healthcare services is one of the best practices for improving search rankings. Google reviews from patients are important to grow your medical practice. I learned about why Google reviews, as well as our practice's Google My Business page, are crucial components of the success of our practice during a recent class about this subject.

Now I will tell you that one of my FAVORITE things is responding to incorrect Google reviews! First, let me clarify that if we did something wrong and we need to deal with it, we will. But I don't think that it is fair that people are having to run their business out of fear that Karen is going to 1-star review you. As I have already stated, I take the football back and I go on offense.

Two of my favorite such instances are when I fired a woman who was incidentally having an affair with a married man. So, he hops on Google and 1-star reviews me and starts calling me out by name. He started sharing some private health information that he would have only been able to have known about because of the pillow talk that was obviously occurring between my former employee and himself. My reply went something like this:

Dear J.B.-

I can only presume that this incognito name that you left on my review is to hide your real identity. I can only presume that you are the married man who my former staff member is sleeping with. Please remind her that sharing confidential and protected health information is a violation of federal law and she is still under that jurisdiction even though she is not under our employ anymore.

Warm Regards,

Mark

"J.B." quickly removed his negative review.

I recently had a 1-star review and the patient was mad that she hadn't come for 5 years and we were charging her a new patient fee again. I took the time to educate the people reading her review of the logical flaws of her bad review, including that she wanted to come back to us after 5 years gone. I told her I was going to go to Sonic and get drinks for the whole office to celebrate them doing their jobs well and for this 1-star review. We posted photos of our 1-star party. Complete with a single Mylar helium balloon. (Photos to follow)

I don't let people pick on us online. I don't have time for it. Again, if we did something wrong, I'll own it, but if you are complaining that we were behind because we worked you into the schedule, you are talking crazy in my book. I fight back and I use humor. People see that we have a sense of humor about ourselves and they are more likely to give us a chance.

If you don't have thick skin, then online reputation management is not for you.

Google reviews from patients are important to grow your medical practice.

ACTION STEPS:

Do you have a repeatable way to get online reviews from your satisfied patients?

Are you asking your patients for reviews?

Is your staff?

Do you have a system in place to turn a negative situation into a positive one?

What is your strategy for dealing with difficult patients who leave bad reviews?

If you don't have an answer for these questions, then you need to develop a plan. Your online reputation is too important to leave to chance.

D 5 reviews

★ ★ ★ ★ ★ a month ago

Very upsetting that i used to see Dr Sam. Last visit was in 2017. Today i called to book an appointment but said hes not taking new patients and since its been so long that im considered a new patient so they wouldnt accept my appointment with Dr Sam.

 Like

Response from the owner a month ago
Hey   I'm going to go ahead and break down this review for those who are reading this and realizing that you actually aren't rating us a 1-star.

1) If we REALLY were a 1-star organization, you wouldn't have wanted to come back to us and been upset that Dr. Sams is no longer able to accept "new" patients. For the record, it is the insurance world that dictates the definition of a "new" patient and not us. Your 5 year absence classified you as a "new" patient.

2) Though you didn't mention this, if we really were a 1-star organization, we wouldn't have offered you a very capable (and well rated, I might add) Chiropractor who would have seen you.

3) If we really were a 1-star organization, Dr. Sams wouldn't be sought out by people all over the world (yes, I literally mean the world) for his level of care in nutrition, acupuncture, and other therapies.

For those reading this, Dr. Sams actually does take new patients, but just not any new Chiropractic patients as his focus has become more Functional in nature.

          I'm glad we were able to help you in the past. I'm sorry that you didn't take the opportunity to be treated by the highly qualified Doctor you were given the option of seeing instead of Dr. Sams. I'm sorry you decided to lash out at us on Google because you didn't get your way.

There are times when a negative review comes in and we have a staff meeting to correct an issue, but NOT this one   I'm going to make a Sonic run this afternoon to say "Well Done Staff... Thanks for growing, helping, taking care of people, and doing your job!" If I can find a single star balloon, I'm going to get it so we can celebrate that a patient from 5 years ago still wanted to come see us. Thanks for the encouragement!

One of these days, I hope that Google lets businesses review people. If so I would definitely give you 5-stars. Yes, I said 5-stars... for entitlement.

One of our Google 1-star reviews and my reply

Healing Arts Center
August 10 · 🌐

We got a 1-star google review yesterday. Though I don't find Google the appropriate channel to complain, when necessary we make corrective actions... However this review was worth celebrating (which I told the reviewer we would) so today, we threw a "1-star review party" complete with Sonic and a star balloon (only 1 of course).

Thanks for continuing to trust Healing Arts Center with your healthcare needs!

Facebook evidence of our 1-star party!

CHAPTER 29

Celebrating Your Patients

When we all think of medical offices and patients having a great "win," our minds are always taken to the image of the cancer patient standing in the hallway ringing "the bell." Once again, the oncology world has won the marketing game! They created this symbol of accomplishment that everyone wants to accomplish. A goal, if you will, that one must obtain!

I am, in no way, minimizing what the cancer patient has or is going through. I'm just saying that I think other people have the right to celebrate their wins, especially at your office! I realized years ago this fact: The worst thing a person has gone through, is the worst thing that person has gone through. That seems simple, but it is really profound. We cannot compare success based upon the diagnosis, we can only compare it to what that patient has ever experienced in their life. I know I will get grief from my women readers on this, but it's like the pain of childbirth compared to man-flu. Neither person has experienced the other so we cannot actually compare. Instead, let's celebrate!

Let's look at some ways in which to celebrate some patient wins, but also bring attention to the great work that your office is doing. See what I did there? I turned this into a marketing chapter!

GRADUATION DAY

When a patient has completed their full plan of care in therapy, we have a graduation celebration. We get a written testimonial from them, we give them a t-shirt, and we take a picture with them and their therapist. If they grant us permission, we will post their picture and their testimonial on our "graduation wall." I remember after my wreck when I was in vision therapy, I kept looking at that wall, and I kept asking, "How do I get up on the wall?" They told me I would have to complete my plan of care and then I could graduate to the wall. That cheezy graduation certificate and the picture I have with that doctor is something I will treasure, because I know how hard it was to attain!

One additional thing we do with their written testimonial form is we add that to their discharge paperwork and we fax that to the referring provider so he or she can read (in the patient's own hand) how we helped them.

HALLWAY OF FAME

This is another way to show off some success stories as well as make the patient feel appreciated. Simply put up a picture of the patient (with their permission) in the hallway with a short blurb about their success story.

PATIENT APPRECIATION DAY

This is something you should do at least annually in your office. Get out the grill and make some hamburgers and give out door prizes. It's a great way to show your patients how much you appreciate them coming to see you. While they are there, do a "Free Screening" to check on their progress to see if you need to get them back on your schedule. Sometimes your local bank will have a grill on wheels you can "rent" for free.

PATIENT OF THE MONTH

Every month, choose a patient that has made significant progress in their therapy and feature them on your website and social media. This is a great way to show off your success stories as well as make the patient feel appreciated.

"NOW I CAN"

I saw at a job fair last year an office that has these dry erase boards that they have patients write on and hold in front of them underneath a logo of the office. It just says: "NOW I CAN...." The patient then writes what they can now do that they couldn't do before they came to that office. Examples: "Now I can... play with my kids." "Now I can... pick up a grandchild." "Now I can... tie my shoes." You get the idea. This is an awesome way to show off the success of your patients in a very visual way!

REVIEWS AND REELS

I know I keep talking about this, but get them to celebrate their wins publicly on social media and give you a "shoutout" or a review. TikToks or Instagram Reels are a great way for someone to social influence others for your practice.

PODCAST

We are starting a podcast called "Stories of Hope" where we will feature a weekly patient AND their provider to tell their story. This also lets my providers get out of their comfort zone and get in the public eye.

ACTION STEPS:

What are some other ways that you celebrate your patients' success?

What are some ways above that you might want to integrate into your practice?

How can you utilize those great stories to market your practice?

Check out https://info.mysocialpractice.com/social-consent-form-download

Mark Scribner
July 12, 2016 ·

So today was a great day! Almost 14 months after my wreck, I graduated from a very life-changing rehab. Today I completed my neuro-optometric rehabilitation at MVP: Movement, Vision, Performance! I really appreciate Dr. Ashley Reddell and her staff for not giving up on me nor my healing. I am most grateful to God for the near miraculous healing that has been taking place in my life over the past month!

The process of healing and rehabilitation typically is a team effort! I appreciate the Doctors, Nurses, and Therapists who have walked (and are continuing to walk) this journey with me.

BTW- This "graduation" now means I can go back to driving ANYTIME (at night again) and ANYWHERE (back on the Interstate)!   I'm like a caged bird set free!

My Graduation!

CHAPTER 30

The SW's

Though this is a short chapter, it is one you need to read and think about. Changing your mindset on how you view a patient can revolutionize how you agonize over a patient and their decisions that might be against your advice. We call them the SWs.

It's pretty simple:
Some Will
Some Won't
So What
Someone's Waiting

You'll save yourself a lot of grief if you can keep these four points in mind when dealing with patients. Let's look at each one briefly.

Some Will: Some patients will take your advice and make the changes you think are necessary.

Some Won't: This is probably the majority of cases, unfortunately.

So What: You have to accept that you can't save everyone and that not everyone will make the decisions you think are best for them.

Someone's Waiting: Remember that there are other patients who need your help.

It can be frustrating when patients don't take our advice, but we have to remember that ultimately it is their decision to make.

As a doctor, you are always looking out for the best interests of your patients. You want them to be healthy and happy, and you will do everything in your power to make that happen. However, sometimes it can be difficult to convince patients to make the right decisions for their health. They may be reluctant to change their lifestyle or take certain medications. It is important to remember that, at the end of the day, it is their decision to make. However, if you can convince them to make the right choices, they are more likely to stick with those decisions and see better health outcomes as a result.

WHAT YOU CAN DO

There are a few things you can do to try to convince your patients to make the right decisions for their health. First, try to appeal to their logic. Explain why it is in their best interest to make certain choices. Second, try empathizing with them. Put yourself in their shoes and understand why they may be hesitant to make certain changes. Finally, emphasize the importance of ownership. It is their decision, and they need to be prepared to live with the consequences—good or bad.

You always want what is best for your patients. Sometimes, that means convincing them to make tough decisions that they may not be comfortable with. However, if you can explain why those decisions are necessary and help them understand the importance of ownership, they are more likely than not to make the right choices for their health.

But at the end of the day, you can sleep well because you gave it your best and the decision is theirs, not yours.

My brother and I are notorious for caring too much about a decision that someone else is making. He pointed something out to me about this the other day. He said, "Ask yourself this question. Am I more irritated (or happy) than the person who has the most to lose (or gain)?" If the answer is yes, then you are probably caring too much about the outcome. Obviously, if you are the one with the most to gain (or lose) it's a different scenario.

I thought that was pretty good advice and it really fits in well with the SWs.

My last thoughts on the SWs is be careful to not let patients manipulate you because "they spend a lot of money here." Over the years, we have had some patients who spend a lot of money at our practice, they then try to get away with stuff that they shouldn't. We have to be careful not to let them take advantage of us because they are "good" patients. So What... Someone's Waiting.

ACTION STEPS:

1. Don't sweat the small stuff. Not every patient is going to make the decisions you want them to, and that's okay.

2. Focus on the patients who are willing to take your advice and make positive changes.

3. Remember that everyone has different motivations and perspectives, so try to empathize with your patients.

4. Ultimately, it is their decision to make. The best you can do is provide them with the information and support they need to make the best choice for their health.

CHAPTER 31

Investing In Your Staff

You might not think of it this way, but your staff is your most valuable asset. They're the ones who interact with patients day in and day out, and they play a big role in shaping patient perceptions of your practice. So, it stands to reason that if you want to improve your practice, you need to invest in your staff. But how?

We operate a AAAASF Inspected Medicare facility and because of that, we have to keep a record of the meetings we have with our staff. There is a sign-in sheet at many meetings. I then have to sign the bottom of the sheet as an administrator. I feel like I am signing my name ALL THE TIME. I have meetings, and meetings before the meetings, and meetings after the meetings, and meetings because of the meetings. I used to despise all of these meetings, but then I realized just how important these meetings are.

I realized that if I can devote my time to the people working for me and that time can make them more productive, it is going to inevitably make the company more money. I also realized that if I don't have a good relationship with the people working for me, they are going to be less likely to want to do their best work. These meetings are important because they allow me to get to know my staff on a personal level and build relationships with them.

I encourage you to have regular meetings with your staff. Not only as a group, but individually as well. I always tell my staff that I want them to succeed in life. That means not only professionally but personally as well. I want them to make good money. I want them to be good parents. I want them to be a good spouse. I want to be excited when they are excited and sad when they are sad.

TRAINING AND DEVELOPMENT

One of the best ways you can invest in your staff is by providing opportunities for training and development. This could take the form of regular continuing education sessions, bringing in guest speakers for special lectures, or sending staff members to relevant conferences. Not only will this help your staff stay up-to-date on the latest developments in their field, but it will also show them that you're invested in their professional growth. And when your staff feel supported and valued, they're more likely to be productive and engaged.

I have also noticed how much doctors and providers love to have initials after their names for certifications and specialties. Encouraging them to get those certifications, helping them pay for them, and celebrating them when they do can engender great company and professional pride.

REGULAR MEETINGS

Another way to invest in your staff is by communicating with them regularly. Hold monthly or quarterly meetings so that everyone is on the same page about where the practice is going and what their roles are in helping to get there. This is also a great opportunity to solicit feedback from staff about what's working well and what could be improved. When employees feel like their voices are being heard, they're more likely to be motivated and invested in their work.

Here are the meetings I have on the regular:

- Weekly Staff - All clerical/support staff. First thing Monday morning before the office opens. This gets everyone on the same page.
- Weekly Physical Therapy - The entire PT department. We talk about trends, coding, patient care, personal and professional wins, and even specific patient care.
- Weekly meeting with Director of Physical Therapy before the Physical Therapy Meeting - The Director of Physical Therapy and I meet the day prior to the PT meeting to go over the previous week. I specifically devote that time to her. I help her through problems, frustrations, and personnel issues. I also hold her accountable to professional and personal goals she has set.
- Impromptu weekly meetings with the Medical Department - These are not scheduled, but I stay on this department like a fly on honey. Why? Because this department has the ability to hemorrhage cash if not properly managed.
- Monthly Provider Meetings - All providers meet during lunch once a month. We talk about goals, upcoming events, specific departments, growth/decline, staffing, and more. We also laugh a lot during these meetings.
- Semi-Annual All-Staff Meetings - These are the meetings where we officially talk about hand-washing, PPE, bodily fluid clean-up, and other fun policies and procedures that we are required to review annually. The people leading this meeting do a good job of making it "fun."
- Lunch - Don't underestimate the amount of relationships that can be developed during this time. We have a lunchroom that many of the staff eat in. I typically won't eat until after this time so I can just go talk to my staff about life.

ACCOUNTABILITY PARTNERSHIPS

If you really want to see a difference in your staff's productivity, try pairing them up with accountability partners. Every week or two, have employees meet with their partners to set goals and track progress. This could be anything from seeing a certain number of patients per day to completing all charting by the end of each shift. Having someone to hold them accountable will help employees stay focused and motivated, leading to improved productivity overall.

PHYSICAL THINGS

Now, I'm mostly just talking about non-financial investments into your staff in this chapter, but make sure they have a good physical environment that they are working in. Sit in their chair sometime and see how uncomfortable it is. Make sure their chair mat doesn't need fixed. Is their computer slow and glitchy? Would a cordless phone allow them to multi-task more? These are some immediate financial investments that can show you care as well as help them be more productive.

Last year, we had some "excess money" that the owner wanted to invest back into the practice. I got to meet with every member of the staff and get their wish list. It was everything from a new stapler, to some therapy items, to a $10,000 drop table, to a vacuum cleaner, to a tub of Thera putty. I loved playing Santa those days when their wish lists were delivered.

They say in the Midwest that getting someone a drink from Sonic is saying "I love you." A Starbucks run or a morning smoothie for the staff are always welcome investments.

ASSISTING THEM PERSONALLY

Don't underestimate how helping your staff personally can really pay off. Things I have done for my staff:

- Created them an LLC for a side-hustle
- Paid some of their electric bill on a really cold winter
- Delivered them some soup when they weren't feeling well

- Driven them to the hospital at night
- Gone to court with them for a custody battle
- Helped pay some legal fees
- Helped them get a mortgage
- Helped them negotiate with the IRS for some previous tax issues
- Changed their flat tires
- Counseled them through some tough marital times
- Thrown them parties
- and we have gone through LOTS OF KLEENEX while talking about things in life they are struggling with.

Our current staff would almost all attest that this is the best place they have ever worked and the best job they have ever had. I can only presume that some of this is because we have invested in them.

INCENTIVIZING THEM

Don't be afraid to throw some legal financial goodwill at your employees for doing a job well done. Create competitions with prizes. Give them gas gift cards. Don't forget that these people are investing in YOUR retirement plan. Make sure you are taking care of them along the way.

When it comes down to it, investing in your staff is essential if you want your practice to run smoothly and efficiently. By providing opportunities for training and development, holding regular meetings, and establishing accountability partnerships, you can show your staff that you value their contributions—and reap the benefits of a more engaged, productive workforce as a result.

ACTION STEPS:

What meetings are you having regularly?

What meetings do you need to have more regularly?

What physical things at the office do you need to upgrade to help your staff?

What training and development do you want your staff to have?

Who do you know that can give that to them?

How can you show your staff that you appreciate them...this week?

CHAPTER 32

Giving Hope and Helping Patients Live a Life in All Its Fullness

I've already told you that I have a religious background and regardless of where you stand on that, I want to relay a concept that can be converted across many beliefs. The concept is that as a provider, your #1 goal is to help your patient live a life in all its fullness. That philosophy comes from the Bible in the book of John, but let's see how we can apply that to our practice and life.

As doctors, you are charged with helping patients not only in their body, but also in their soul, mind, and spirit. By attending to the whole person, you can give hope and help your patients live a life in all its fullness.

I've heard that one of the most rewarding aspects of being a doctor is having the opportunity to help patients not only in their physical health, but also in their emotional and mental well-being.

As doctors, you are often bombarded with negativity. It can be easy to forget that you have the power to change lives for the better. Every day, you have the opportunity to give hope and help patients live a life in all its fullness. There are many ways that we can do this, but some of the most important include:

Listening: One of the best things that we can do for our patients is to simply listen. In order to understand what they are going through, we need to connect with them on a personal level. This allows us to better understand their needs and how we can best help them. We have found that listening to the "ever since" part of the story helps us diagnose them much quicker.

Providing Support: Patients often need someone to lean on during difficult times. As their doctor, you can provide this support by offering words of encouragement and hope. You can also provide practical support by helping them navigate the healthcare system and connect with resources that can help them on their journey to recovery.

Fostering Hope: One of the most important things that you can do for your patients is to foster hope. This means helping them see beyond their current situation and believe that a better future is possible. You can do this by sharing stories of other patients who have overcome similar challenges, highlighting progress that they have made, and offering words of encouragement.

- In body: You can help by alleviating pain and suffering through your medical care.
- In soul: You can provide comfort and companionship as you listen to your patients' concerns.
- In mind: You can ease anxiety and worry by providing information and education.
- In spirit: You can give hope by sharing your own faith journey with your patients.

I remember an ENT that I used to go to in Lawrence, KS who would end the visit with a "moment of silence." He would say, "I have a religious background, and I believe in the power of prayer. I am going to pray for you in this moment of silence." I thought that was pretty cool that he did that. He didn't push it on anyone nor did he pray out loud. He just sought help from something higher than himself.

At the end of the day, your goal as doctors should be to help your patients live a life in all its fullness. This means giving them hope when they are facing difficult challenges and helping them not only physically, but also emotionally and mentally. By taking the time to truly connect with your patients, you can make a lasting impact on their lives.

ACTION STEPS:

1. Make it a point to connect with your patients on a personal level. This can be done by simply listening to their stories and concerns.

2. Offer words of encouragement and hope. Help them see beyond their current situation and believe that a better future is possible.

3. Seek help from something higher than yourself. This could be done by praying for your patients or sharing your own faith journey with them.

4. Help patients navigate the healthcare system and connect with resources that can help them on their journey to recovery.

5. Take the time to truly connect with your patients. This will make a lasting impact on their lives.

CHAPTER 33

The Best Hire of Your Life

You have made it to the end! Thanks for hanging with me over the past many chapters. I hope you have learned something. I hope this has given you a boost of energy that you can do this. I'm a capitalist at heart and I believe that you will never be sorry for working hard and then letting your hard work, money, and efforts do the work for you. I hope you at least were able to take one nugget from here that can help you scale your practice!

For the scrappers here, this is all you needed—a simple guide to tell you how to make money. For others reading this, you like the concepts, but you need some help implementing these ideas. Maybe you need a me?

Your practice might be big enough and you are risk tolerant enough to do what Dr. Sams did and find someone like me to "run your practice." If that is you, then I want to leave you with this: Make sure you trust that person with your life! Literally. Because the decisions I make on a regular basis could greatly affect the livelihood of Dr. Sams. We have a history. He trusts me, and most importantly, I have never done something to make him lose that trust in me.

A couple of years ago, Dr. Sams and Tricia were headed to work when their car slid off the road and rolled down an embankment about 50 feet off the road and about 20 feet down. They were hanging upside down by their seatbelts. Dr. Sams gathered his wits and tried to dial 911. The phone wouldn't connect so he called me. Tricia, while hanging upside down, started yelling at him and says, "Why are you calling Mark and not 911?" He replied, "Mark is my 911." You need that kind of person in your life!

Every year I step back and make sure that I have earned or saved the company greater than my salary that year. This is a gratifying experience that I only share with myself every year, but it is an exercise that I love doing.

For those of you who aren't able to swing that kind of a risk currently, maybe you need to hire a coach or consultant to help you through the next part of your scaling/growth journey.

Too often, we are afraid to hire a coach because that would mean we were admitting we couldn't do something, that we needed help. I'm here to tell you that is the furthest thing from the truth! As an entrepreneur, your ability to delegate and outsource is one of the biggest indicators of success. It allows you to focus on your zone of genius and continue to grow in that area.

When you are hiring a coach or consultant, you are hiring someone to help you do the things you can't or don't want to do. You are also hiring someone with knowledge and expertise that you may not have.

There are a few things I always make sure of when hiring a coach or consultant:

1. Hire someone who has done what you want to do. There is no substitute for experience. Plus, I think it is important to hire someone who is ACTUALLY CURRENTLY DOING what you are doing. I'm

so tired of young doctors who are "no longer in practice" trying to stay relevant and market to me to help "grow your practice like I did."

2. Make sure they are a good fit personality-wise. You will be spending a lot of time with this person so you want to make sure you mesh well.

3. Check references! This is so important. Make sure you talk to other people who have worked with this person to get a feel for what it is like to work with them.

4. Set clear expectations. This is important for both parties. Make sure you are clear on what the coach or consultant will be doing and that they are clear on what you expect from them.

5. Have a clear end date. Nothing is worse than working with someone who you feel is just milking the clock. Set a clear end date from the beginning so that both parties are aware of when the work will be done.

Hiring a coach or consultant can be a big win for you personally, professionally, and financially.

I've shown you some things that we have done well, and not-so-well that we were able to learn from. If ever our company could help you take that next step, reach out to me at:

Practice Fixers
www.practicefixers.com
mark@practicefixers.com

We can help your practice with any of the areas addressed in this book through consulting, mentorship, coaching, referrals, and more.

We love to help practices and doctors take those next steps because we are here ***with you in the trenches***. We just happen to be a few steps ahead.

To close in a paraphrase of fictional Coach McGinty...

I look at you and I see two people: the person you are and the person you oughta be. Someday those two people will meet, and it should make for one heck of a doctor and one heck of a medical practice.